Mastering Self-Leadership

THIRD EDITION

Mastering Self-Leadership

Empowering Yourself
for Personal Excellence

Charles C. Manz

University of Massachusetts, Amherst

Christopher P. Neck

Virginia Tech

PEARSON
Prentice
Hall

Upper Saddle River, New Jersey 07458

Library of Congress Cataloging-in-Publication Data

Manz, Charles C.
  Mastering self-leadership : empowering yourself for personal excellence /
Charles C. Manz, Christopher P. Neck. — 3rd ed.
    p. cm.
  Includes bibliographical references and index.
  ISBN 0-13-140046-0 (alk. paper)
  1. Leadership. 2. Self-actualization (Psychology)   I. Neck, Christopher P. II. Title.

HD57.7M387 2003
303.34 — dc21

2003043858

Acquisitions Editor: Michael Ablassmeir
Editor-in-Chief: Jeff Shelstad
Assistant Editor: Melanie Olsen
Editorial Assistant: Kelly Wendrychowitz
Executive Marketing Manager: Shannon Moore
Marketing Assistant: Patrick Danzusa
Managing Editor (Production): John Roberts
Permissions Supervisor: Suzanne Grappi
Manufacturing Buyer: Michelle Klein
Cover Design: Bruce Kenselaar
Cover Illustration: PhotoDisc, Inc.
Composition/Full-Service Project Management: Jennifer Welsch, BookMasters, Inc.
Printer/Binder: Courier Westford

Credits and acknowledgments borrowed from other sources and reproduced, with permission, in this textbook appear on appropriate page within text.

Pearson Education LTD.
Pearson Education Singapore, Pte. Ltd
Pearson Education, Canada, Ltd
Pearson Education–Japan

Pearson Education Australia PTY, Limited
Pearson Education North Asia Ltd
Pearson Educación de Mexico, S.A. de C.V.
Pearson Education Malaysia, Pte. Ltd

10 9 8 7 6 5 4 3 2 1
ISBN 0-13-140046-0

To Karen, Mom, and Dad
the three people who contributed the most
to my acquisition of self-leadership
sufficient to write this book.
CM

To Jumper and Dr. Patin,
who showed me that
my only limitations
are those that I place
on myself.
CN

Brief Contents

Contents

Preface

"Argue for your limitations and sure enough, they're yours."
— RICHARD BACH

History provides numerous examples of successful people who were confronted with many "can'ts" in terms of making their dreams come true.

- **Sandra Day O'Conner**, the first woman on the U.S. Supreme Court, could not get a job as a lawyer on graduating from law school. The only job offered to her was that of a legal secretary.
- **Michael Jordan**, arguably the best basketball player of all time, was cut from his high school basketball team.
- **Ludwig van Beethoven**, one of the world's major composers, was told by a music teacher that he had no talent for music. In fact, this teacher once remarked about Beethoven, "As a composer he is hopeless."
- As a young man, **Walt Disney**, the great cartoonist and movie producer, was advised to pursue another line of work by a newspaper editor in Kansas City: "You don't have any creative, original ideas."
- A Munich schoolmaster told 10-year-old **Albert Einstein**, who later became a brilliant scientist, "You will never amount to much."
- In 1962, Decca Recording Company turned down the opportunity to work with an unknown music group called **The Beatles**. Their rationale was "We don't like their sound and guitar music is on the way out." This unknown singing group subsequently became a legendary group of musicians.
- **Dr. Seuss's** first children's book, *And to Think That I Saw It on Mulberry Street*, was rejected by 27 publishers. The 28th publisher, Vanguard Press, sold 6 million copies of the book.
- The book *Chicken Soup for the Soul*, written by **Jack Canfield** and **Mark Hansen**, was turned down by 33 publishers before Health Communications agreed to publish it. All the major New York publishers said, "It is too nicey nice" and "Nobody wants to read a book of short little stories." Since that time, more than 80 million copies of the *Chicken Soup for the Soul* series have been sold worldwide, with translations in 39 languages.
- In 1935, the *New York Herald Tribune's* review of **George Gershwin's** classic *Porgy and Bess* stated that it was "surefire rubbish."
- **Thomas Edison**, the inventor of the electric light, the phonograph, and more than a hundred other useful items, was told by a teacher that he was too stupid to learn anything.
- During their first year in business, the **Coca-Cola Company** sold only 400 bottles of Coke.
- In response to **Fred Smith's** term paper proposing reliable overnight delivery service, a Yale University management professor wrote, "The concept is interesting and well formed, but in order to earn better than a C, the idea must be feasible." Smith went on to establish Federal Express Corporation, based on the ideas in this "average" paper.
- Inventor **Chester Carlson** pounded the streets for years before he found backers for his Xerox photocopying process.

- Before he founded Apple Computer Incorporated, **Steve Jobs** was rejected by Atari and Hewlett-Packard during his attempt to get interest in his personal computer idea. Hewlett-Packard personnel remarked, "Hey, we don't need you. You haven't gotten through college yet." Jobs thus pursued the idea himself, and Apple's first year's sales exceeded $2.5 million.

- In December 1977, with only $20,000 to his name, **Michael Burton** was laughed at by colleagues and bankers when he quit his lucrative small business consulting job and vowed to turn his snowsurfing concept into a popular sport. By 1998, however, Burton was owner of Burton Snowboards, the largest pure snowboarding company in the world, with annual sales of more than $150 million. Due to Burton's promotional efforts, snowboarding is enjoyed by 8 million people worldwide, and it officially became a medal sport in the 1998 Winter Olympics. Who's laughing now?

These are just a few illustrations of people who persevered—who led themselves by using their strengths, skills, and determination to overcome the "can'ts" in their lives—who in their mind knew they could do it. They did not let initial failures rob them of their dreams. They followed their inner voices and kept forging ahead until their fantasies became realities.

What is your dream? Is it perhaps to become a doctor? A lawyer? A supermodel? A CEO? Is it to start your own business? To raise a healthy and happy family? To become a teacher? A rock star? A television news anchor? Maybe you want to win an Academy Award? Possibly even become president of the United States? Despite what some may try to tell you, whatever you want to become, you *can!* As William A. Ward once wrote,

> *If you can believe it, you can achieve it;*
> *If you can dream it, you can become it.*

Do you believe in yourself and your ability to make your dreams come true? We hope this book provides you with the skills to lead yourself toward living your goals and dreams. We hope our words solidify your belief in your potential and abilities, so that you can achieve and become whatever you desire. Most of all, we hope the knowledge within the following pages will help you to travel the paths of Michael Jordan, Walt Disney, Dr. Suess, Albert Einstein, and others. These individuals believed that the impossible was possible, that the unthinkable was thinkable, that the undoable was doable. These remarkable individuals *thought* they could; these go-getters *knew* they could! Hopefully, this book will help *you* lead yourself to personal excellence, too!

Acknowledgments

As with most worthwhile projects, a great many people have contributed to this book. In particular, we would like to thank Hank Sims, Greg Stewart, Bob Marx, Vikas Anand, Peter Hom, Heidi Neck, Rhonda Reger, Greg Moorhead, Bryan Dennis, Jeff Houghton, Jeff Godwin, Robert Ashcraft, Mike Goldsby, Wanda Smith, Charles Koerber, Krishna Kumar, and Stuart Mease for their collegial support of us and our work over the past several years. Chuck Manz also wants to thank those individuals who helped shape his early thoughts on the issue of self-leadership, including Art Bedeian, Kevin Mossholder, Bill Giles, Kerry Davis, and Denny Gioia.

We gratefully acknowledge the special inspiration we have received from the work, ideas, and thoughtful encouragement of Richard Hackman, Ed Lawler, Chris Agryris, Fred Luthans, Ted Levitt, Rosabeth Moss Kanter, Richard Walton, John Kotter, Kenneth Cooper, Tom Thompson, Tedd Mitchell, Brent Neck, Sherry Petta, Damian Luckett, and Dick Heinrich. We would like to offer special thanks to the authors who contributed sidebars to this edition, including Vikas Anand, Carl Fey, Karen Manz, Robert Marx, Tedd Mitchell, Craig Pierce, Henry P. Sims, Jr., Greg Stewart, Tom Thompson, Stuart Mease, David Moore, and Paul Tiedt.

We also would like to recognize our respective universities—University of Massachusetts at Amherst (especially the Isenberg School of Management) and Virginia Tech (especially the Pamplin College of Business)—for supporting our research and writing. Our thanks extend to our deans and chairs: Tom O'Brien, Richard Sorensen, Bill Wooldridge, and Jon Shepard. Charles Manz truly thanks the generosity of Charles and Janet Nirenberg, who funded the Nirenberg Chair of Business Leadership, the position he holds at the University of Massachusetts. Chris Neck would especially like to thank the thousands of students at Virginia Tech and Arizona State University who inspired and encouraged him to test and develop many of the ideas presented in this book. Further, he would like to thank the Management Department Staff (especially Sandy Crigger) for their assistance during the past 8 years.

Chris additionally would like to acknowledge the kindness of the fine people at PowerBar. Specifically, Alyssa Berman and Shannon Ratay are thanked for believing in his teaching philosophy and supporting his teaching approach.

In addition, we want to express our appreciation to the Prentice Hall team for their assistance in converting our ideas into a book. We want to especially thank David Shafer, Jeff Shelstad, and Bill Beville for their above-and-beyond assistance toward making this book a reality.

We want to express our gratitude to our families for their patience during our long hours under lamplight writing away. We especially want to thank our wives, Karen and Jennifer, who positively shaped the contents of this book through their listening, guidance, encouragement, and understanding. As with most things in our lives, Karen and Jennifer made this book better by their magic touch!

Finally, Chuck Manz would like to thank Mike Mahoney, who helped provide the direction and shape to his growing desire to explore the realms of the vast potential locked in each living person—especially those who have the good or bad fortune to have to work for a living. Chris Neck would like to thank Dr. Joseph Patin for the encouragement and support during those "killer" runs together many years ago and for helping him believe in his ability to lead himself.

About the Authors

Charles C. Manz, Ph.D., is a speaker, consultant, and best-selling business author. He is currently the Charles and Janet Nirenberg Professor of Business Leadership in the Isenberg School of Management at the University of Massachusetts. Dr. Manz's work has been featured on radio and television and in *The Wall Street Journal, Fortune, U.S. News & World Report, Success,* and several other national publications. His work has been translated into several languages including Japanese, Swedish, Spanish, Indonesian, Korean, Chinese, Portuguese, and German. He received the prestigious Marvin Bower Fellowship at the Harvard Business School, which is "awarded for outstanding achievement in research and productivity, influence, and leadership in business scholarship."

Dr. Manz's previous books include *Business Without Bosses: How Self-Managing Teams Are Building High-Performing Companies* (Wiley, 1993, 1995), a selection of the Fortune Book Club and translated into several foreign languages; *SuperLeadership: Leading Others to Lead Themselves* (Prentice Hall, 1989; Berkeley, 1990), winner of the Stybel-Peabody national book prize, an Executive Book Club selection, and translated into several foreign languages; *Mastering Self-Leadership: Empowering Yourself for Personal Excellence* (Prentice Hall, 1999); *Company of Heroes: Unleashing the Power of Self-Leadership* (Wiley, 1996), a featured selection of the Executive Book Club; *For Team Members Only: Making Your Workplace Team Productive and Hassle-Free* (Amacom, 1997); *The Leadership Wisdom of Jesus: Practical Lessons for Today* (Berrett-Koehler, 1998), which is featured on audiotape and translated into several foreign languages; and *Teamwork and Group Dynamics* (Wiley, 1999). His four newest books include *The New SuperLeadership: Leading Others to Lead Themselves* (Berrett-Koehler, 2001), *The Wisdom of Solomon at Work: Ancient Virtues for Living and Leading Today* (Berrett-Koehler, 2001), *The Power of Failure: 27 Ways to Turn Life's Setbacks into Success* (Berrett-Koehler, 2002), and *Emotional Discipline: The Power to Choose How You Feel* (Berrett-Koehler, 2003).

Dr. Manz has served as a consultant for many organizations, including 3M, Ford, Motorola, Xerox, the Mayo Clinic, Procter & Gamble, General Motors, American Express, Arthur Andersen, Allied Signal, Unisys, Josten's Learning, Banc One, the American Hospital Association, the American College of Physician Executives, the U.S. and Canadian governments, and many others.

Dr. Christopher P. Neck completed his Ph.D. in Management at Arizona State University. He is currently an Associate Professor of Management at Virginia Tech. He received his M.B.A. from Louisiana State University. Dr. Neck is author of the books *Medicine for the Mind: Healing Words to Help You Soar* (McGraw-Hill, 1997), *For Team Members Only: Making Your Workplace Team Productive and Hassle-Free* (Amacom Books, 1997), *Mastering Self-Leadership: Empowering Yourself for Personal Excellence* (Prentice Hall, 1999), and *The Wisdom of Solomon at Work: Ancient Virtues for Living and Leading Today* (Berrett-Koehler, 2001). His research specialties include executive/employee health/fitness, self-leadership, leadership, group decision-making processes, and self-managing team performance. He has published more than 60 articles and chapters in various journals and books. Some of the outlets in which Dr. Neck's work has appeared include *Organizational Behavior and Human Decision Processes, The Journal of Organizational Behavior, The Academy of Management Executive, Journal of Applied Behavioral Science, The Journal of Managerial Psychology, Executive Excellence, Human Relations, Human Resource Development Quarterly, Journal of Leadership Studies, Educational Leadership*, and *The Commercial Law Journal*.

Due to Dr. Neck's management expertise, he has been cited in numerous national publications including *The Wall Street Journal, The Washington Post, The Los Angeles Times, Entrepreneur Magazine, Runner's World*, and *New Woman Magazine*. Additionally, as a faculty member at Virginia Tech, Dr. Neck teaches a management practices course to a single class of more than 550 students. He has received numerous teaching awards at Virginia Tech including the 1996, 1998, 2000, and 2002 Outstanding Teacher of the Year Award (voted by the students for the best teacher of the year within the entire university), and the 2002 Wine Award for the outstanding teacher at Virginia Tech (voted by faculty and students).

Some of the organizations that have participated or have scheduled to participate in Dr. Neck's management development training, self-leadership training, and keynote speeches include GE/Toshiba, Busch Gardens, Clark Construction, the U.S. Army, Crestar, American Family Insurance, Sales and Marketing Executives International, America West Airlines, American Electric Power, W.L. Gore & Associates, Dillard's Department Stores, and Prudential Life Insurance.

Finally, Dr. Neck is an avid runner. He has successfully completed 12 marathons including the New York City Marathon and the San Diego Marathon.

Mastering Self-Leadership

CHAPTER

The Journey

1

It is not easy to find happiness in ourselves,
and it is not possible to find it elsewhere.

— AGNES REPPLIER

"I can do it!" he shouted at the figure across the room. "All my life you've been holding me back, beating me down — I've had it! Why? Why can't you just let me be? I could really be somebody," he continued, now in a pleading voice.

For a while he was quiet except for the sound of his own deep breathing. He just stared at what he now realized was his ultimate adversary. The figure was still; it said nothing. "Oh, God," he sighed. He shifted his gaze to the bright lights of the city below. Beginning to see the possibilities for his life, he felt a surge of excitement, of potential purpose, go through his every fiber.

He was lost somewhere in his imagination for what seemed several minutes. Suddenly reality hit him squarely and coldly again. His sense of possible escape was lost. He felt the chains weighing heavy on his soul. And he returned his gaze slowly, steadily, helplessly to the figure of his oppressor. Once more he looked squarely into the eyes of the figure in the mirror before him.

This book will encourage you to "look into the mirror." It emphasizes that we choose what we are and what we become. It recognizes that the world does not always cooperate with our goals, but that we largely create that personal world with which we must cope. It also points out that we influence our actions in countless ways, of which we might not even be aware.

The world is experiencing a knowledge explosion. It is frightening to realize that what we learn often becomes obsolete in a short time. What doesn't change, however, is our need to deal effectively with this complex world and to lead ourselves to fulfillment in life. If we can develop the ability to renew ourselves continually and to overcome our obstacles on our way to life's exhilarations, we can become what we choose for ourselves.

LEADERSHIP

This book is not about leadership of others. Instead, it is about something more fundamental and more powerful — *self*-leadership. It is about the leadership that we exercise over ourselves. In fact, if we ever hope to be effective leaders of others, we need first

1

to be able to lead ourselves effectively. To understand better the process of self-leadership and how we can improve our capability in this area, it is useful first to explore the meaning of the term *leadership*.

Leadership has a seemingly endless number of definitions and descriptions—largely as a result of the vast number of persons who have researched and written about the subject (and the equal vastness of their different viewpoints). One widely recognized name associated with the topic is the now-deceased Ralph M. Stogdill. Dr. Stogdill authored a handbook of leadership, published in 1974, which reviewed theory and research on the subject. Since that time, this book has been revised by Bernard M. Bass, most recently in 1990.[1] The book has pointed out that leadership has been conceived of in many ways, including the art of inducing compliance, a personality concept, a form of persuasion, a set of acts or behaviors, an instrument of goal achievement, an effect of group interaction, a differentiated role, and the exercise of influence. All of these descriptions have some merit. The most useful definition of leadership—to focus on the idea of self-leadership—however, is simply "a process of influence." This short definition is a broad and meaningful one that recognizes the importance of human influence in determining what we are and what we do and the complexity involved. (Influence takes place not as an isolated event, but as a process involving many parts.)

The existing literature on leadership focuses almost universally on influence exercised by one or more persons over others (in other words, influence exercised by "leaders" on others). The first step involved in undertaking a journey toward achievement of an understanding and improvement of our own self-leadership is recognizing that leadership is not just an outward process; that is, we can and do lead ourselves.

SOURCES OF LEADERSHIP

Leadership (the process of influence) can originate from a number of sources. The most commonly recognized source of leadership involves the influence leaders exercise over their followers. This is also the most externally oriented view of leadership. It does not recognize the influence that we exercise on ourselves. An example of this external view is the giving of orders and the use of other methods of influence (such as rewards and punishments) by a formal organization manager over his or her subordinates.

A pictorial representation of different sources of leadership follows (see Figure 1-1). It depicts leadership as ranging from an entirely external influence process at one extreme to a self-imposed process at the other. The latter focus is the primary topic of this book. Between these two extremes, leadership influence consists of different combinations of external influence and self-influence. When a goal is set jointly by a manager and a subordinate, a participative leadership process is at work.

At this point, we are ready to take the next step of our journey; that is, the journey into ourselves toward the realization that we do lead ourselves.

WE ALL LEAD OURSELVES

Even in the most highly controlled situations, we influence our behavior in various ways. If you have a boss who gives you detailed orders and frequently checks your progress (and probably is not too shy to let you know what you're doing wrong), you

BEFORE BEHAVIOR — — — — · **BEHAVIOR** — — — — **AFTER BEHAVIOR**

examples:
    setting goals
    giving orders
    encouragement
    expectations
    threats

examples:
    rewards such as praise,
    money, promotion

    punishments such as verbal
    reprimand, dismissal, demotion

EXTERNAL LEADERSHIP

Charlie, I want to see efficiency increased by 10% in your department—go to it, I know you can do it.

Efficiency up by 12%—great job Charlie. I've recommended you for a promotion.

PARTICIPATIVE LEADERSHIP

Charlie, I think we need some improvements around here.

I agree. How about shooting for a 10% increase?

I know—we need to increase our efficiency.

That sounds reasonable.

Efficiency up by 12%—great job Charlie. I've recommended you for a promotion. Let me know if there is anything else I can do for you.

You've got it.

Well, I'd like to take that vacation I've been putting off.

SELF LEADERSHIP

We need some improvements around here. I think I'll try to increase efficiency by 10% in my department. I can do it.

Fantastic! Efficiency is up by 12%—I knew I could do it. I think I'll take that vacation I've been putting off—I've earned it.

FIGURE 1-1   Sources of Leadership

still possess a great deal of discretion. The method or order in which you complete tasks, for example, is left to you. What you think about while you work is also up to you. If you choose to set a higher or lower personal goal for yourself than what your boss expects, that too is up to you. You can feel good about your progress or be tough on yourself for even the smallest of mistakes if you choose.

The point is that you are your own leader much of the time. Even if you are faced with influential external leaders, they are not likely to be staring over your back every minute. In their absence, who is in charge? You are, of course. Even if they are present, they cannot look into your mind. In fact, we are our own ultimate leaders. We are capable of negating anything we hear externally and substituting our own internal communication. (Example—From boss: "You're loafing, and what little work you *are* doing is poor quality." To self: "Everyone around here knows I'm the best worker in our department—obviously, the boss is being unreasonable today.")

Consider the following story.

On a construction site in the Southwest, when the lunch whistle sounded, all the workers would sit together to eat. Every day Joe would open his lunch pail and start to complain. "Gosh darnit," he'd cry, "Not again—a bologna sandwich and corn chips." Day after day, week after week, Joe would moan and groan and say, "Not again, a bologna sandwich and corn chips."

Weeks passed and other workers were getting tired of his complaining. Finally, one of Joe's fellow construction workers said, "C'mon Joe, what's your problem? Every day you complain about your bologna sandwich and corn chips, so, for Pete's sake, who in the heck makes your lunches?"

Joe replied, "I do."

What the story suggests is that what we do with our lives, including where we work and for whom we work, is largely left to us. In other words, we make our own lunch. If we need more training to obtain the kind of job we really want, it's up to us to lead ourselves to make the kinds of sacrifices necessary to achieve our ends. We are not trying to say that it's an easy process. In fact, to lead ourselves to do what we really want is difficult, but it can be done if we know how to go about it.

Belief in your ability to "make your own lunch"—that is, to lead yourself—can be a life or death matter. A recent study in *The Lancet*, a British medical journal, revealed that a feeling of little or no control at work explains why rank-and-file employees (civil service employees) have a greater risk of heart disease (50 percent higher) than that of top management. This book can provide you with the tools to lead yourself, to gain a feeling of more control in all aspects of your life, and thus to reduce the risk of such helpless feelings.[2]

We all lead ourselves. This is not to say that we are all effective self-leaders. On the contrary, we all have weaknesses in our own self-leadership process. In some people the process is dysfunctional. Many lead themselves into the wrong line of work and into the wrong job; even more lead themselves into unhappiness and discontentment with their lives. Perhaps the saddest of all are those who give up much of their self-leadership potential to others and are led into equally negative conditions. The point is that you are your own leader, and just like any leader you can be a good one or a bad one. In the pages that follow, we attempt to help you understand your self-leadership patterns and how to improve them. The ideas you choose to adopt for yourself, however, are up to you. After all, you are your own leader.

SELF-LEADERSHIP

Building on the definition of leadership presented earlier in this chapter, self-leadership can be described as "the process of influencing oneself." This definition is general and does not provide the detail necessary to gain a better understanding or a more effective execution of the process. It does point out, though, the global target at which this book is focused—the process that we experience in influencing ourselves. The primary elements of this process will be presented and discussed throughout the remainder of the book. First, however, we attempt to summarize, in a general sense, the primary ingredients of self-leadership.

The concept of self-leadership is derived primarily from research and theory in two areas of psychology. The first, *social cognitive theory*,[3] recognizes the adoption and change of human behavior as a complex process with many parts. It recognizes that we influence and are influenced by the world we live in (more on this idea in Chapter 2). The theory places importance on the capacity of a person to manage or control oneself—particularly when faced with difficult yet important tasks. (This viewpoint serves as the primary basis for Chapter 3.) Social cognitive theory also recognizes the human ability to learn and experience tasks or events through vicarious and symbolic mechanisms (which points out the importance of our ability to learn by observing others and to use our imagination). Chapter 5 addresses these ideas more fully. Finally, the social cognitive theory stresses the importance of our perceptions of our own effectiveness or potential to be effective (more on this in Chapter 8).

The second important area of knowledge for this book can be described as *intrinsic motivation theory* (and even more specifically as *cognitive evaluation theory*).[4] This viewpoint emphasizes the importance of the "natural" rewards that we enjoy from doing activities or tasks that we like. The ideas included in the writings on intrinsic motivation point out the potential to harness the motivational forces available in doing things that we can really enjoy. (Chapter 4 addresses these ideas.)

The knowledge included in these two insightful areas concerning human behavior represents the major foundation for this book. Ideas also will be borrowed from other bodies of knowledge, including motivation theory and leadership theory. Overall, this book will recognize the importance of forces that we use to influence ourselves (often without being aware of them) and the potential for altering our worlds so that they are more motivating to us. At this moment, to help you visualize the concept of self-leadership and its application to your life, please ponder the following poem:

Leading the Band
He was going to be the President
Of the U.S. of A.
She was going to become an actress
In a Broadway play.
As youngsters—these were their dreams;

The visions they aspired to.
They truly thought these aspirations,
Eventually, would one day come true.
But he did not become President.
The reason is the ultimate sin.
He never ran for office.
He feared he would not win.
She didn't make it to New York City.
In fact, never set a foot on the stage.
She thought she'd forget her lines.
In other words—she was afraid.
The lesson in these stories
Is that you must get up and try.
If you let your fears control you,
Your dreams will quickly die.
Because if you want to hit a home run,
You have to go up to the plate.
If you want to meet that special person,
You have to ask them for a date.
The biggest crime in life
Is to forget what you have dreamt.
It's not the act of losing
But to have never made the attempt.
So as you battle with your fears in life,
Remember this brief command:
"If you're not afraid to face the music,
You may one day lead the band."

SOURCE: Christopher Neck, *Medicine for the Mind: Healing Words to Help You Soar* (New York: McGraw-Hill, 1996).

In short, the goal of this book is to develop a framework capable of helping you motivate yourself to achieve your personal goals—to help you "lead the band" in your personal and professional lives. The journey has begun—lead onward.

Notes

1. Ralph M. Stogdill, *Handbook of Leadership* (New York: Free Press, 1974); and Bernard M. Bass, *Bass and Stogdill's Handbook of Leadership* (New York: Free Press, 1990).
2. As reported in *USA Today*, 25 July 1997.
3. See Albert Bandura, *Social Foundations of Thought and Action: A Social Cognitive Theory* (Upper Saddle River, NJ: Prentice Hall, 1986).
4. See, for example, Edward Deci and Richard Ryan, "The Empirical Exploration of Intrinsic Motivational Processes" in L. Berkowitz (ed.), *Advances in Experimental Social Psychology* 13, 1980; and Richard M. Steers, Lyman W. Porter, and Gregory A. Bigley, *Motivation and Leadership at Work* (New York: McGraw-Hill, 1996): 496–502.

Mapping the Route

2

or We Do Choose

*The wisest of insights that can be gained by any man or woman
is the realization that our world is not so much what it is
but what we choose it to be.*

—STATEMENT MADE BY A WISE INDIVIDUAL—

OR IF IT WASN'T, IT SHOULD HAVE BEEN.

A number of years ago I, C. Manz, worked as a retail clothing salesperson during a Christmas holiday break from college. One particularly hectic day, I observed a woman, amidst a mob of customers, looking through piles of casual slacks. She was obviously frustrated and grumbled as she worked her way through the piles. I had been straightening the pants between helping what seemed to be an endless onslaught of customers, and I noted that the woman's method of searching was, much to my dismay, essentially to destroy slacks by throwing them on the floor or stuffing them in other piles as she continued her search. Finally, she turned to a customer nearby and commented, in obvious displeasure, that the slacks were in a totally disorganized mess, and she could not find the size she needed. At this point, being a bit tired and irritable myself and having watched her undo a substantial amount of my work, I turned to her and said, "You know why they're a mess, don't you?" She looked at me, obviously surprised, thought for a few moments, then said, "I suppose because of impatient, pushy ladies like me."

Many of us practice the same kind of behavior throughout our lives, and, unfortunately, it often concerns considerably more important matters. For example, the way we behave toward others will largely determine the way they behave toward us. We can alienate people and then complain (just as the woman did in the clothing store) about the mess our relationship is in. It is important to realize, though, that we do impact our world just as it impacts us. We change the world just by being alive. We breathe the air, we take up space, we consume limited food resources, and so on.

We may even bring out the hostility in others just by being alive. I, C. Manz, recall quite vividly an experience that I had when I was about 16 years old. I was walking down a long hall in my high school, thinking of nothing in particular, when I heard an

7

exasperated sigh behind me. I turned around to receive a lethal look from a girl in my class and to hear the words "would you get out of my way?" snapped at me. It turned out that this young lady wanted to walk faster than I and had tried several times (unsuccessfully, given the crowd of students in the hall) to pass me. By the time I realized that she was competing for my physical space, my existence as a living being had already made her angry. Most of us probably can offer similar examples of experiences in crowded restaurants or traffic jams.

We have little control over the impact we have on the world in cases such as these. What is of greater importance is the behavior that we freely choose to practice. What we choose to do with our lives and how we go about accomplishing our chosen ends will largely shape the relevant world in which we live. To appreciate the importance of this idea, several issues need to be addressed. The first concerns the substantial impact that the world has on us.

EXTERNAL FACTORS

The world we live in *does* influence what we do with ourselves on a day-to-day basis and can largely shape our ultimate destiny in life. Considerable evidence has been gathered from many different organizations that reveals the important impact that being rewarded has on chosen actions.[1] In fact, one author has gone so far as to write "On the Folly of Rewarding A, While Hoping for B,"[2] suggesting that what we are rewarded for is the type of behavior that we are likely to use even if some other behavior is more desirable. The point is that we respond to what we experience and especially to what we receive for our efforts.

Being rewarded for what we do can influence what we choose to do in the future. This is because rewards provide us with information concerning what leads to positive or negative results and incentives to do what is rewarded. We are more likely to do in the future those things that we anticipate will lead to desirable results and not do those things we expect to lead to negative results. This logic is simple and widely supported by research.

Many influences affect our daily living. Laws place limits on our choices, as do rules that we must follow to function within organizations. If we violate these limits, negative results are likely to follow, such as getting traffic tickets or being dismissed from our jobs. The intention of this book is not to suggest that external influences such as these are not important; rather, it is to emphasize the important role we play in determining the external influences that will be relevant to us. Also, it is to emphasize the importance of influences that we place on ourselves directly. The world does impact our lives, but we are in no way helpless pawns.

PERSONAL FACTORS

Each person is unique. We all possess certain qualities, ways of thinking, and so forth that help determine how we see the world and what we do with our lives. To understand fully our own self-leadership practices, we must recognize the importance of what we are and how we think about things. This book is particularly concerned with our personal differences in terms of the actions we choose. Rather than dealing with abstract concepts such as "attitudes" or "values," a more workable approach is to deal with individual behaviors.

A broad view of the concept of "behavior" is needed to understand self-leadership. Behavior takes place at an observable physical and an unobservable mental level. In fact, the events that come before behavior and the results of behavior take place at these same physical and mental levels. Thus, complex chains of behavioral influence take place. This idea is represented pictorially in Figure 2-1. For example, imagine a person who thinks about the joys of trout fishing and decides to skip work that day but later feels guilty. This example includes a mental event (thinking about fishing) that comes before and influences an actual physical behavior (skipping work). The physical behavior is followed by a mental result (guilt), which is likely to discourage similar behavior in the future.

The way we practice self-leadership is affected by our unique tendencies in terms of thinking patterns and our physical action. We can lead ourselves to desired accomplishments by combining these two levels of influence.

To illustrate these ideas further, let's use a cereal box endorsement as an example. Lance Armstrong is a cancer survivor and three-time winner of the premier bicycling event in the world, the Tour de France. This event consists of 20 stages over 22 days averaging more than 100 miles per day. Armstrong recently appeared on the front of a cereal box with the caption "Breakfast of Champions." One might conclude from this statement that Lance Armstrong's motivation for training centered on winning the Tour de France and thus becoming the champion cyclist in the universe. In actuality, if

FIGURE 2-1   Mental and Physical Levels of Influence

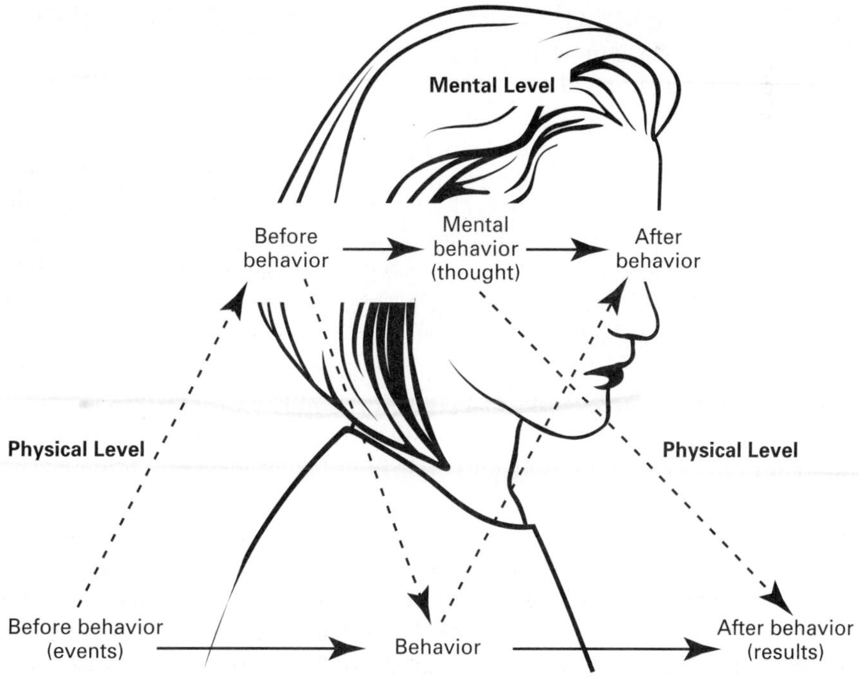

he just threw himself into the training through force of will, basing his only motivation on the reward of winning the Tour de France, what he actually would get would be physical and mental pain, blisters, cramps, sore legs, dehydration, and other consequences that most of us would not view as rewarding at all. The victory in this prestigious race is a worthy pursuit, but a great deal of self-leadership is needed to carry a person through the sacrifices necessary to reach that final destination.

Physical and mental forces are involved in maintaining this level of motivation. For example, Lance Armstrong could compete in smaller events and win awards and recognition on the way to the "yellow jersey." (A yellow jersey is awarded to the victor of the Tour de France.) He also could mentally picture the moment of victory—arms raised as he crosses the finish line of the final stage of this race and perhaps doing cereal endorsements if he chooses to do so. By taking actions (mental and physical) such as these, he can maintain the necessary level of motivation to complete the difficult training.

The Lance Armstrong example highlights the importance of achieving the level of motivation needed to make difficult sacrifices. This type of self-leadership will be discussed more fully in the next chapter. Self-leadership also can capitalize on the attractiveness of doing things that we like to do. (For Lance Armstrong, it might be the natural enjoyment of activities such as endurance cycling.) This aspect of self-leadership will be dealt with in a later chapter. First, however, this chapter deals with the mutual influence among persons, their behavior, and their world—and especially the importance of the choices we make.

WE DO CHOOSE

We as persons, our behavior, and the world in which we live are closely related. Each of these factors places important influences on the others.

For example, our behavior helps determine what we will be faced with in our world. If our actions generally contribute to the well-being of those we come in contact with, positive forces for a more favorable, relevant world are put into motion. By taking such actions, we can help ensure the personal security and happiness of others and also increase the likelihood of their being supportive of us. On the other hand, if our actions are strictly for our own benefit at the cost of others, we might get what we want in the short run but in doing so create a hostile world in which we must live in the longer run. Ebenezer Scrooge creates for himself this sort of hostile world in Charles Dickens's *A Christmas Carol*.

The influence the world has on our behavior is also important, as noted earlier in this chapter. Thus, our behavior and our world influence one another. Indeed, Scrooge takes actions that largely create a hostile world for himself, which likely brings out more hostility in Scrooge. A vicious cycle of influence is set into motion, which eventually requires the appearance of frightening ghosts so that Scrooge's own behavior breaks the cycle.

A final factor that needs to be included to complete the influence picture is ourselves. Because this book is concerned with behavior as a workable focus for improving our own self-leadership, a useful way of viewing ourselves is in terms of behavioral predispositions. That is, the concern is not with elusive ideas like "good attitudes" or "bad attitudes," but instead with what are our behavioral tendencies (physical and mental). This viewpoint is represented by questions such as, "How do we tend to react to certain types of situations?" or "How do we think about problems?" Such tendencies will influence how we behave and how we view the world. (The world is probably more a product of the way we see it than what it really is in any concrete sense.) Also, our behavioral tendencies or predispositions are greatly influenced by what we experience, such as praise from our fellow humans for certain types of behaviors. They also are influenced by past behaviors. Most of us, for example, tend to develop habits and patterns in our conduct. In addition, it has been suggested that if we change our behaviors, a change in us as persons (attitude) will follow.[3]

The mutual influence between each of these factors is represented pictorially in Figure 2-2. The illustration suggests that we as persons, our world, and our behavior cannot be fully understood separately. Instead, each factor continually influences and is influenced by the other. We should not expect to have circumstances work out to our optimum liking just because we behave in a favorable way. Other factors are involved besides the actions we take. At the same time, we do exercise choices that can have a major impact on what we experience and thus increase our chances for more frequent desirable outcomes.

The choices we make concerning all three parts of the total influence picture are important. First, the world includes potential influences that will not affect us unless we allow them to do so. We do not feel the effects of cold weather unless we leave our dwelling and expose ourselves to the cold. Also, you are not affected by this book unless you choose to read it; it is only a potential influence that is dependent on your choice to pick up a copy and make the effort and take the time to read the words it contains.

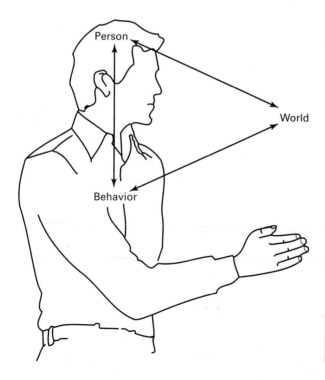

FIGURE 2-2   The Three Factors of the Influence Picture

We also choose the actions we take that in turn influence the world. For us, the ideas we had on self-leadership were only a potential influence for the world until we took the time and made the effort to write this book. If our choosing to write this book helps others become more effective and contented, then our world is that much improved.

We also can have a choice in how we think about what we experience. For example, we can decide to take an optimistic view of the world, even though many others take a pessimistic one. In doing so, we have accomplished two things. First, our world is going to look more positive to us and as a result will be a more enjoyable place to live. Second, as a result of choosing to take an optimistic view of things, we may respond more to the opportunities of life rather than to its constraints. Thus, to the extent that we can choose what we are as a person (or at least the way we practice thinking about things), we can influence what the world is to us and how we behave toward it.

The point is, even though we function within a complex system of influence— involving ourselves, our behavior, and our world—we possess a great deal of choice concerning what we experience and what we accomplish with our lives. We are subject to constraints. These include limitations in our situations (for example, because of Earth's gravity we cannot fly without the aid of equipment of some kind) and the roles in which we find ourselves (such as parents, bosses, citizens). This fact, however, is no reason to feel helpless. Even when faced with the most difficult situations, we lead ourselves by the choices we make.

To clarify this point, consider the plight of two frogs.

> Two frogs fell into a bucket of cream. The first frog, seeing that there was no way to get any footing in the white fluid, accepted his fate and drowned.
>
> The second frog didn't like that approach. He thrashed around and did whatever he could to stay afloat. Soon his churning turned the cream into butter, and he was able to hop out.

The point is that both frogs were faced with a challenging situation—falling into a bucket of cream. Indeed, they both led themselves by the choices they made. One led himself to his death because he chose to let his "world" control him. The other frog led himself to safety because he adapted to his world; he controlled what he was able to control— himself—by working hard to reach safety. Both frogs practiced self-leadership; however, only one frog did it effectively.

To further illustrate the importance of choice, let's look at an example that involves a rather troubling situation. Imagine that you are the head of a group. The group could be a department in a company, a community organization, or whatever else might seem relevant to you. In this group, you are faced with a troubling individual. This person always complains at the smallest hint of being slighted. To stop these annoying occasions, you have found yourself giving in to his wishes much as a parent might to a whining child. This might involve giving him special privileges that others do not have, or doing things his way even if his way makes things difficult for everyone else. Over time, you have fallen into a pattern without recognizing it until finally the situation becomes nearly intolerable. What can you do?

The solution to the problem is simple. The value of presenting it is in illustrating the issue at hand. You simply choose to stop giving in to the complainer. This might lead to rather annoying experiences at first, but gradually the situation (your world) is likely to improve. In the present pattern, you are rewarding this person for complaining and thereby encouraging the situation to continue and even worsen. You also are being rewarded yourself by eliminating the complaining each time it occurs. Thus, until the choice is made to break the pattern and lead yourself out of the situation, your rewarding behavior is likely to increase, which will make the situation worsen.

To cope with the immediate negative effects of excessive complaining when you stop giving in, you need to motivate yourself to stand firm. This could be done by using methods such as mental support (for example, having such thoughts as, "I'm not giving in this time, buster. I know I can stand firm and things are going to improve around here.") or by removing yourself temporarily from the presence of the complainer.

Specific approaches that can be used to lead yourself to do what you set out to do are discussed in the following chapters. The lesson at hand is that we do choose. We do not live in a vacuum that is free from all external forces. Would life be interesting if we did? We are faced with challenges, obstacles, and many difficult situations. All this makes effective self-leadership that much more important and rewarding. We are self-leaders—why not be the best ones we can be? Travel onward and see if you can lead yourself to this end.

Notes

1. See, for example, M. P. Heller, "Money Talks Xerox Listens," *Business Month* (September 1990): 91–92; and W. Clay Hammer and Ellen P. Hammer, "Behavior Modification on the Bottom Line," *Organizational Dynamics* (Spring 1976): 3–21.

2. Steven Kerr, "On the Folly of Rewarding A, While Hoping for B," *Academy of Management Journal* 18 (1975): 769–783.

3. Arnold P. Goldstein and Melvin Sorcher, *Changing Supervisor Behavior* (New York: Pergamon Press, 1977).

Rough Roads, Detours, and Roadblocks

or Leading Ourselves to Do Necessary but Unattractive Tasks

> *Hard work won't guarantee you a thing,*
> *but without it you don't stand a chance.*
> —PAT RILEY

"I can't face another—no, not today," she groaned to herself as she looked at her new formidable challenger.

"You must," she heard from a voice somewhere in the deep recesses of her mind. Only moments before she had overcome what she thought to be her last adversary of the day and had risen to start the journey she had longed for—only to be challenged again. Looking cautiously at the massive features of the beast, she sighed deeply in dismay. But then a strategy came to her and her determination returned. She reached swiftly, but with great control, for her weaponry. Flipping the appropriate switches on the dark rectangle before her, she swung it open. The beast seemed almost to shrink from the sound alone. Then she reached efficiently, coolly, for the mechanism with the illuminated dial and the powerful lance that she knew together could overcome the beast . . . she braced herself . . . then, without warning, she was upon it.

Some hours later she backed away wearily, victoriously, from her defeated, now harmless-looking, prey. She had won again but wondered how much longer she could endure such battles. She sighed, stretching and rolling her shoulders, while momentarily closing her eyes. Then slowly, the finished report before her, she returned her calculator and pen to her briefcase and rose for her journey to the suburbs.

Let's face it—it's not always easy to do the things that we know we should. Often the sacrifices and effort necessary to reach our desired destinies and to become fulfilled as people present formidable barriers. So how do we lead ourselves over the rough roads of our life's journey? How do we motivate ourselves to hang in there when everything seems to be saying, "Give up, you fool—you can't do it"?

Our inner nature might be likened to a constant battle between opposing forces. A part of us seems to say, "Give up; take the easy way out; it's just too difficult; don't even try." Another part of us seems to say, "I want my life to count for something; I want to become all that I am capable of becoming." So how do we get ourselves to take action and do the things that we believe we should do? How do we get ourselves to face life's hardships and lead ourselves to our own personal victory, to our own chosen destiny? Indeed, in many ways we experience the inner conflict of a Dr. Jekyll and Mr. Hyde. How do we lead ourselves to win the battle that Dr. Jekyll lost?

This chapter is about leading ourselves to do unattractive but necessary tasks. It's about leading ourselves to face the challenges, make the sacrifices, and take the necessary actions to achieve what we choose for ourselves. We suggest specific strategies for managing our own behavior. These strategies are especially suited for motivating and leading ourselves in the face of difficult and, at least in the short run, unappealing but necessary tasks (undesirable desirables).

Take a few moments to assess some of your own self-leadership tendencies. Respond to the self-assessment questionnaire shown in Table 3-1 by circling the number corresponding to the description (e.g., describes me very well, describes me well, and so on) that you believe best reflects your position regarding each of the statements included. Some of the statements (1 through 18) might seem a bit redundant. Try not to let this bother you. Respond to each statement and score your responses according to the directions provided. You might want to indicate your responses and calculate your score on a separate sheet of paper. That way you can reuse the questionnaires and exercises included in this book at a later date without being biased by your earlier responses.

Interpreting Your Score

Your score for A through F suggests your current self-leadership tendencies concerning six self-leadership strategies that will be addressed in this chapter. Your score for each of these strategies could range from 3 (a total absence of the strategy in your current behavior) to 15 (a very high level of the strategy in your current behavior).

Your score on A through F can be interpreted as follows:

1. A score of 3 or 4 indicates a *very low* level of the strategy.

2. A score of 5 to 7 indicates a *low* level of the strategy.

3. A score of 8 to 10 indicates a *moderate* level of the strategy.

4. A score of 11 to 13 indicates a *high* level of the strategy.

5. A score of 14 or 15 indicates a *very high* level of the strategy.

Evidence indicates that the use of each of these strategies tends to be related to higher performance, with the exception of self-punishment (E). Therefore, a high score on A, B, C, D, and F reflects a high level of self-leadership, which is likely to enhance

TABLE 3-1 Self-Leadership Questionnaire 1 (SLQ1)
Self-Assessment Questionnaire for Dealing with Unattractive but Necessary Tasks

	Describes Me Very Well	Describes Me Well	Describes Me Somewhat	Does Not Describe Me Very Well	Does Not Describe Me At All
1. I try to keep track of how well I'm doing while I work.	5	4	3	2	1
2. I often use reminders to help me remember things I need to do.	5	4	3	2	1
3. I like to work toward specific goals I set for myself.	5	4	3	2	1
4. After I perform well on an activity, I feel good about myself.	5	4	3	2	1
5. I tend to get down on myself when I have performed poorly.	5	4	3	2	1
6. I often practice important tasks before I actually do them.	5	4	3	2	1
7. I usually am aware of how I am performing on an activity.	5	4	3	2	1
8. I try to arrange my work area in a way that helps me positively focus my attention on my work.	5	4	3	2	1
9. I establish personal goals for myself.	5	4	3	2	1
10. When I have completed a task successfully, I often reward myself with something I like.	5	4	3	2	1
11. I tend to be tough on myself when I have not done well on a task.	5	4	3	2	1
12. I like to go over an important activity before I actually perform it.	5	4	3	2	1
13. I keep track of my progress on projects I'm working on.	5	4	3	2	1
14. I try to surround myself with objects and people that bring out my desirable behaviors.	5	4	3	2	1
15. I like to set task goals for my performance.	5	4	3	2	1
16. When I do an assignment well, I like to treat myself to something or an activity I enjoy.	5	4	3	2	1
17. I am often critical of myself concerning my failures.	5	4	3	2	1
18. I often rehearse my plan for dealing with a challenge before I actually face the challenge.	5	4	3	2	1

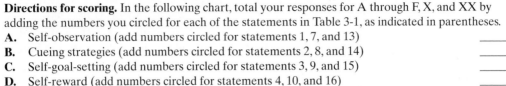

TABLE 3-1   (Continued)

Directions for scoring. In the following chart, total your responses for A through F, X, and XX by adding the numbers you circled for each of the statements in Table 3-1, as indicated in parentheses.

A.   Self-observation (add numbers circled for statements 1, 7, and 13)   _____
B.   Cueing strategies (add numbers circled for statements 2, 8, and 14)   _____
C.   Self-goal-setting (add numbers circled for statements 3, 9, and 15)   _____
D.   Self-reward (add numbers circled for statements 4, 10, and 16)   _____
E.   Self-punishment (add numbers circled for statements 5, 11, and 17)   _____
F.   Practice (add numbers circled for statements 6, 12, and 18)   _____
X   Total score, including self-punishment (add scores for A through F)   _____
XX   Total score, not including self-punishment (add scores for A through F, except E)   _____

your performance. A high score on E, however, reflects a high level of self-punishment, which might detract from your performance. Each of these strategies is discussed in more detail throughout the remainder of the chapter.

Your score on X indicates your overall use of the self-leadership strategies, including self-punishment. Your score could range from a low of 18 to a high of 90. Your score on X is not easy to interpret because it includes self-punishment, which might detract from performance. Your score on XX, on the other hand, reflects your score on only the five self-leadership strategies which, in general, are positively related to performance (your score could range from 15 to 75). Your score on XX can be interpreted as follows:

1. A score of 15 to 22 indicates a *very low* overall level of the strategies.
2. A score of 23 to 37 indicates a *low* overall level of the strategies.
3. A score of 38 to 52 indicates a *moderate* overall level of the strategies.
4. A score of 53 to 67 indicates a *high* overall level of the strategies.
5. A score of 68 to 75 indicates a *very high* overall level of the strategies.

A high score on XX usually suggests that you already possess some positive self-leadership tendencies. Regardless of your score, this chapter is designed to help you implement and improve upon several self-leadership techniques that are available. A high score on the questionnaire indicates that you believe you are exercising these self-influence methods. Whether you are using them or using them *effectively* is a different matter.

The field of psychology has recently provided some interesting discoveries regarding means we use to control our own behavior. The area of thought that has come to be called *self-control* or *self-management* is especially insightful.[1] Several useful techniques for getting ourselves to do the "undesirable desirables" are suggested by the work in this area.[2] Some of the strategies that are available are addressed in the questionnaire you have just completed and will be discussed in the remainder of the chapter. These strategies can be classified under two general approaches: strategies that alter the world and the way it impacts on us in a beneficial way, and strategies that we directly impose upon ourselves to influence our own behavior. By reading the remainder of this chapter, you will gain insight on how to implement these strategies more fully and effectively into your own self-leadership. Guidelines will be offered, including checklists that summarize the primary steps involved, as well as exercises to help you get started in practicing systematic self-leadership.

WORLD-ALTERING STRATEGIES

We possess the ability to make alterations in our immediate worlds that will help us behave in desirable ways. Many of these alterations are simple, yet they allow us to make a real difference in our actions. Three different strategies will be offered here.

Reminders and Attention Focusers

"What's this piece of paper with a big letter A on it doing on your office door?"

"It's to remind me to buy my wife flowers for our anniversary. I forgot last year, and if I forget again she'll skin me alive."

This first strategy involves using physical objects to remind us of, or to focus our attention on, things we need to do. Probably the most well-known example of this strategy is tying a string around one of our fingers to remind us of something. Admittedly, if we used this method today we probably would be met with amusement and embarrassing comments from coworkers and friends. Other similar methods are available that offer practical benefits.

One simple strategy that has been emphasized for improving the effectiveness of our management of time is to make a list of our pending tasks.[3] At the beginning of a workday, for example, make a list of all the important things that need to be done during the day. If possible, prioritize the list and keep it handy throughout the day. The list not only serves as a reminder and guide but also can provide the basis for a feeling of personal accomplishment and reward as items are crossed off the list.

Many additional techniques are available. For example, if we have a top-priority project that needs to be done, we can place it in the center of our work space. When we return to our work area, we have a powerful reminder of our most pressing task. The important point is that we can use physical cues to focus our efforts. The challenge is to find those reminders and attention focusers that work best for us and use them.

Removing Negative Cues

Every time we go to that restaurant, I am overcome by the dessert display. For the good of my diet, can't we go somewhere else for lunch today?

If we wish to eliminate our behaviors that we don't like, one strategy is to eliminate cues that might lead to these behaviors. If we wish to cut down on our consumption of sweets, we can remove the candy dish from the coffee table. Similarly, if we are disturbed about excessive time spent watching television, we can move the TV set to another less frequently used room.

The point is that we are surrounded by physical cues that tend to encourage certain behaviors. If we can identify the things in our world that encourage our undesired behaviors, then we can remove or alter them. In addition, we can remove ourselves from their presence. If we need to get some work done, for example, we are well advised to leave the TV room or game room (with all their powerful cues) and go to a study room. In fact, we can design the layout of the rooms in our homes with healthy, constructive living in mind. Similarly, we can design our work space to eliminate cues to destructive, unproductive behavior.

Increasing Positive Cues

I think placing the safety record displays around the plant has had positive results. It keeps our workers thinking about safety, and our accident record has improved.

Another strategy involves increasing the cues that tend to lead to positive behaviors. If we would like to become more knowledgeable on a particular subject but find that we never take the time to read much on that subject, what can we do? We can set up cues that will encourage our reading. We could, for example, place appropriate books on a table next to our favorite chair. We might then be faced with a choice between cues for reading and some other activity such as watching television (if we have not removed the TV set), but at least we are more aware of the choice.

We also can arrange cues that impact on important matters—such as what kind of a person we can become. The workplace, for example, contains many important cues for desired and undesired behavior. If our workplace contains more negative cues than positive ones, we can try to alter the cues available or if not, perhaps it's time to make a job change.

Coworkers can serve as powerful cues. Are their values consistent with yours? Over time, coworkers are likely to influence what we become. If we know ourselves, what we are striving toward, and what we believe in, it is important to surround ourselves with the right people. We are likely to select role models from among our associates. Do your present role models display behaviors that are consistent with the achievement of what you have chosen for yourself? If we work with people whom we view as using unethical means to achieve their ends, we are exposing ourselves to undesirable cues. On the other hand, we can choose to associate with persons who act in consistent ways with our values and who successfully achieve the worthwhile ends we desire. By choosing such an organization and consequently the people who work there, we establish positive cues for our behavior.

The following checklist is provided to summarize the major steps for exercising self-leadership through the use of world-altering (cues) strategies. The primary objective of the strategies is stated first, and a list of the primary steps involved follows. (Note: This general format will be adopted in all the checklists throughout this book.)

Using the checklists provided throughout this book as a guide, make a list of additional steps that would be helpful to you. In addition, an exercise is provided to help you get started in applying these techniques.

CHECKLIST FOR USING CUES

Use cues to help you exercise self-leadership.

- Use physical cues to remind you of your important tasks—for example, make lists to guide your daily activities.
- Establish cues to focus your attention on important behaviors and tasks—for example, place helpful signs around your work area that focus your thinking in desired ways.

(continued)

- Identify and reduce or eliminate negative cues in your work environment—for example, remove objects you find distracting.
- Identify and increase positive cues in your work environment.
- Wherever possible, associate and surround yourself with people who cue your desirable behavior.

CUES EXERCISE

Study how cues affect your behavior. Make notes.

1. How do you use reminders and attention focusers?
2. What are some ways you could improve on your use of reminders and attention focusers?
3. List some negative cues in your work environment that are encouraging your undesirable behaviors.
4. How might you reduce or eliminate these negative cues?
5. List some positive cues in your work environment that are encouraging your desirable behaviors.
6. How might you increase these positive cues?

SELF-IMPOSED STRATEGIES

In addition to creating or altering cues in our world to influence our own behavior, we can exercise control over ourselves directly. The cement that lays the foundation for this self-imposed control is the information we possess about ourselves—our *self-awareness*. By observing our own behavior and its causes (for example, why we behave in desirable or undesirable ways), we are provided with the necessary information to manage ourselves effectively. Thus, the first self-imposed strategy is *self-observation*.

Self-Observation

> That is the third time I've lost my temper and criticized someone today, and I've done it several other times this week. I wonder what's wrong and why I'm behaving like such an ogre?

Self-observation involves determining when, why, and under what conditions we use certain behaviors. For example, if we feel we are not accomplishing enough each day in our work because of wasted time, we can study the distractions we experience. Are we spending too much time engaged in informal conversations? By observing the amount of informal conversing we participate in and the conditions that exist at the time, we can learn more about this behavior. If 5 hours are spent chatting during the 8-hour workday, we probably have a problem. Furthermore, if most of these conversations begin during a visit to the office water cooler, we have useful information to help us cut down on the behavior (we need to cut down on our trips to the water cooler).

Additional power can be added to this strategy if we physically record our self-observations. A handy pen and a 3″ × 5″ card might be all we need to make brief notes that can be examined in detail later.

Self-observation can provide the foundation for managing our behavior. Several other distinct strategies build on this foundation. It is important to remember that we already use these strategies in our daily living; the problem is that we often use them unknowingly and ineffectively.

A checklist summarizing the major steps for practicing self-observation follows. Also, an exercise is included to help you get started using self-observation.

CHECKLIST FOR SELF-OBSERVATION

Use self-observation as a basis for self-leadership.

- Identify behaviors that you feel are especially important that you would like either to increase or reduce.
- Keep a record of the frequency and duration of these important behaviors.
- Note the conditions that exist when these behaviors are displayed.
- Identify other important factors concerning these behaviors—for example, the time of day or week they tend to occur, or who is present at the time.
- When possible, keep a written record of your self-observations, but try to keep the process simple enough that you will not be discouraged from using it.

SELF-OBSERVATION EXERCISE

Develop your self-awareness.

Intentionally observe yourself for the next week. Make notes about behaviors that you see as desirable and undesirable. Include the frequency and duration with which they occur, when they occur, and why you think they occur (identified reasons for your behaviors should include external world influences and directly self-imposed influences). Develop your own self-observation system for future use.

Behavior	Frequency and Duration	When (Day/Time)	Why (External and Internal Influences)

Self-Goal Setting

If you don't have a destination, you'll never get there.

—HARVEY MCKAY

It is futile to exert effort with no direction. Imagine for a moment that you and some friends decide to take a road trip together, so you all pile into a large van and you are selected as the driver. You start the van and head toward the nearest freeway. For awhile, everyone in the van is happy and smiling. Then about an hour later someone remarks, "Where are we going?"

You reply, "I don't know." Other members just shrug their shoulders. After a few minutes, some bickering erupts among the passengers because someone wants to go to city A, but someone else wants to go to city B. Amid the noise and chaos, you think to yourself, "Wow, this mess could have been avoided if we had reached a mutually agreed upon destination before we left."

Every day you "travel" somewhere. In short, your traveling involves working toward success in your personal and professional life. The question that arises is, "Do you know what you are working *toward?*" In other words, do you know your destination, or are you traveling without a clear picture of where you are going—without specifically knowing what you are trying to achieve?

This story illustrates what can happen to you in your daily activities if you fail to set a destination in terms of what you want to achieve. In other words, your destination is your personal goal. Consider the definition of *goal* as "the *result* toward which your effort is directed."[4] What is the result in which your effort is directed? In short, what are your goals?

One way we can provide ourselves direction in our self-leadership is through the use of personal goals. What we strive toward in terms of our long-term life achievements as well as on a daily basis influences our behavior. Often we are not clear on what our goals are. We might want to achieve a position of importance and influence in life, for example, but we do not determine how we will go about obtaining the position or even what the position will be. The systematic, thought-out, intentional setting of personal goals can influence our behavior positively.

Self-set goals need to address long-range pursuits and short-run objectives along the way. If we decide on a long-range goal of becoming a lawyer, we need to accomplish many shorter-range goals, such as acceptance into law school and passing courses once we are admitted. Our immediate behavior in turn should be pointing at specific short-term, meaningful goals such as reading a law journal (or a few pages in a journal) or completing a law brief (or a portion of a brief). The shorter-range goals should be consistent with the longer-range goals for maximum effectiveness. We must first engage in the necessary self-analysis to understand what we want out of life before we can set the goals that must be reached to achieve these ends. This process takes effort, and although our goals are likely to change over time, it is important that we try to have current goals for our immediate efforts.

Goals are generally more effective for managing our immediate behavior if they are specific and challenging, yet achievable. If we set unreasonable goals that we cannot realistically achieve, we are likely to do more harm than good. Realistic achievable goals, on the other hand, can be satisfying when we reach them.

If we understand what we value in life and what we want to accomplish, then we can set specific, achievable goals (such as reading 1 hour each day on a given subject or attending a lecture to improve our skills in a given area). It is often helpful to record in writing our long-term and immediate goals and then modify them as necessary. We spend a great deal of time doing things with our lives. A little effort expended on setting self-goals can help us have purpose and direction so that we don't waste valuable time.

Successful self-leaders don't travel without a specific goal. If you don't have specific goals, you never get anywhere. Take some time to think about your life and what you want to accomplish—set goals. Following are tips to help you summarize our discussion on goals thus far.

Conduct a Self-Examination

Before you can establish specific goals, you need to decide what's important to you and what you'd like to accomplish (the next section of this chapter should help you conduct this step). You must truly want to accomplish your self-set goals, so you must truly value your final destination. (The goal-setting exercise that follows might help you with this point.)

Avoid Fuzzy Goals—Be Specific

If you say to yourself, "I'll someday be the best employee in the company," you might have a goal, but it's not likely to happen. The problem is the term *someday*. The word *someday* in your goal is fuzzy; it's unclear and nonspecific. Your goal needs to be specific. *When* are you going to be the best employee? *What* does "best" mean? *How* are you going to do this? If your goals are more specific, they paint a more vivid picture of your destination and thus make it easier to get there.

Set Long-Term and Short-Term Goals

Your goals need to focus on the long and the short term. If you decide on a long-term goal of becoming the top performer in the company, you need to accomplish short-range goals to get there—for example, learning new skills or improving current skills. Another way of looking at this is to imagine that your long-term goal is to write a book. To do this, you set a short-term goal of writing five pages each day. Short-term goals help you reach your long-term destination—what you truly value in life or your purpose in life. Indeed, we cannot talk about the benefits and importance of long-term goals without discussing the ever-important concept of "purpose."

Peaking with Purpose

We are focusing on how self-leadership can help in terms of performing necessary but unattractive tasks. In the next chapter, we examine the concept of "naturally rewarding tasks and activities." A central component of a naturally rewarding work process is establishing a sense of purpose. Thus, in the next chapter we emphasize the concept of "purpose" as a strong component of such a work process. However, purpose is also a key aspect of self-goal-setting, especially the self-setting of long-term goals. Consequently, we now begin our discussion of purpose examination.

Think for a moment about the word *purpose*. What does it mean to you? In this chapter, it refers to our reason for being, our aim in life, our reason for getting up in the morning. In short, purpose establishes our ultimate long-term goal(s). Richard Leider, in his book *The Power of Purpose,* describes purpose in the following manner.[5]

Purpose is that deepest dimension within us—our central core or essence— where we have a profound sense of who we are, where we came from, and where we're going.

Purpose is the quality we choose to shape our lives around. Purpose is a source of energy and direction.

Leider suggests that having purpose involves asking ourselves three fundamental questions.[6]

- Who am I?
- What am I meant to do here?
- What am I trying to do with my life?

Have you pondered these questions before? Do you know the answers? The importance of answering these questions is that to be truly happy, you must discover your purpose and then live it! For some people, purpose might be spiritual. For others, it might be work related. For many, it might be a combination of both dimensions. If you don't live your purpose, we believe you will not reach full contentment in your life. You will feel like something is missing. Abraham Maslow stated this point best.

> A musician must make music, an artist must paint, a poet must write, if he is to be at peace with himself. What a man must be, he must be.

Are you happy right now? Do you enjoy your job? If not, perhaps you are in a job that does not help you fulfill your purpose—that does not allow you to use your talents and skills. Are you performing well on your job yet still are not happy? Are you, as someone once said, climbing the ladder to success only to realize that the ladder was propped up against the wrong wall? Have you achieved a plethora of short-term and long-term goals in your life but still you are not content? Then perhaps your ladder in life has been propped up against the wrong wall. Maybe you have been striving to achieve goals that have nothing to do with the wall in your life, with that which really matters to you—your purpose in life. Those individuals who are truly happy and are "peaking" in their lives are those who are performing a job and accomplishing goals that indeed reflect their purpose in life.

The Old Testament serves as an illustration of Maslow's words—that we must live our purpose to be truly self-actualized. To live our purpose is to truly reach our potential, to become everything we are capable of becoming, to become ultimate self-leaders. Consider the following parable from the Book of Judges 9:7–15.

> The trees once went out to anoint a king over themselves. So they said to the olive tree, "Reign over us." The olive tree answered them, "Shall I stop producing my rich oil by which gods and mortals are honored, and go to sway over the trees?" Then the trees said to the fig tree, "You come and reign over us." But the fig tree answered them, "Shall I stop producing my sweetness and my delicious fruit, and go to sway over the trees?" Then the trees said to the vine, "You come and reign over us." But the vine said to them, "Shall I stop producing my wine that cheers gods and mortals and go to sway over the trees?" So all the trees said to the bramble, "You come and reign over us." And the bramble said to the trees, "If in good faith you are anointing me king over you, then come and take refuge in my shade."

Among the many messages underlying this parable, a key lesson involves purpose. Clearly, the olive tree, the fig tree, the vine, and the bramble brush illustrated the words of Maslow. They realized that to reach their potential or peak in life, they must do what they were supposed to do, what they were created to do. They realized that their unique purposes were to produce sweet fruit (the fig tree), rich oil (the olive tree), wine (the vine), and shade (the bramble bush). These trees had discovered their purposes and were intent on living them.

Are you living your purpose right now?

The Search for Purpose

> Purpose is the reason a person was born. From birth to death, each of us is on a quest to discover that reason. Many never do. Yet, our world is incomplete until each one of us discovers our purpose.[7]

Do you know what your purpose is in life? Have you begun your own personal search for your purpose in life? If you have yet to realize your purpose, you are not alone. As Viktor Frankl points out, "Ever more people today have the means to live, but no meaning to live for."[8] If you connect with Frankl's words and do not feel meaning in your life, then the time to start the search might be right now.

As the previous words suggest, the quest for purpose can be a long and difficult one, yet our efforts to explore for a purpose in life are worthwhile. The rewards are immense. The rewards are living a contented life in which we truly believe we are using our gifts to make a contribution to our world.

To clarify this message, consider the mythical legend of the search for the Holy Grail. Although this story has many versions, the basic synopsis is as follows.[9]

> The legend of the Holy Grail is one of the most enduring in Western European literature and art. The Grail was said to be the cup of the Last Supper and at the Crucifixion to have received blood flowing from Christ's side. It was brought to Britain by Joseph of Arimathea, where it lay hidden for centuries. The search for the vessel became the principal quest of the knights of King Arthur. It was believed to be kept in a mysterious castle surrounded by a wasteland and guarded by a custodian called the Fisher King, who suffered from a wound that would not heal. His recovery and the renewal of the blighted lands depended upon the successful completion of the quest. Equally, the self-realization of the questing knight was assured by finding the Grail. The magical properties attributed to the Holy Grail have been plausibly traced to the magic vessels of Celtic myth that satisfied the tastes and needs of all who ate and drank from them.

In this story, the search for the Holy Grail was not an easy task. The knights had to undergo "many perils and trials along the way."[10] The Grail was difficult to find, and only a few knights out of many were able to find it. The knights who found the Grail underwent sacrifice, persistence, struggle, and perseverance but in the end enjoyed much happiness and at the same time were able to help others (e.g., heal the king). Similarly, the search for one's purpose is not an easy mission. It can take years of trial, error, and self-observation to truly discover who we are and what we are supposed to be doing with our life. Those who discover their mission and purpose in life are those who sacrifice, who persist, who persevere until they eventually find it. As in the case of the Holy Grail discovery, those who realize their reason for being not only discover a happier life for themselves, they also are able to make a deeper contribution to society (help others) because they are using their talents to make a difference.

The Importance of Having Purpose in Life

Having purpose is the catalyst for organizing life. Purpose itself can serve as our guide to how to spend our lifetime and how to allocate our resources. If we realize our meaning for existence (our ultimate long-term goal), then every decision we make can be guided by this realization. To clarify, recall the last time you went to the grocery store. Did you bring a shopping list with you? If not, what happened? If you are like many people, when you got home you realized you bought some items that you did not need. Similarly, without a purpose in your life, you can "buy" or accomplish a shopping cart of goals that don't amount to much or that you don't need or want. Having purpose in your life is kind of like having a shopping list at the store. In the grocery store of life, purpose helps you buy only that which is truly important to you. It can help you avoid spending time on things that you don't value.

Spirituality and Work Life: A Search for Purpose and Meaning

—Karen P. Manz and Robert D. Marx

The workplace has changed. Companies are downsizing to improve stockholders' investments. Work is being done more cheaply in foreign labor markets. The idea of company loyalty or security in employment is largely a thing of the past. The resulting insecurity of the workplace has sent people looking elsewhere for meaning and purpose.

Workers have changed, too. Many baby boomers reach middle age and beyond and begin to wonder how they should spend the rest of their lives. What will be their quality of life and legacy? Other, perhaps younger, workers might struggle to find a sense of significance among an increasingly diverse and dispersed workplace.

A new movement, Spirituality and Work Life, has been spawned by our need to find greater meaning in an ever-changing workplace. Books, conferences, courses, and Web sites that help people express their spirit at work have mushroomed.[11] For many, business values that emphasize competition, profitability, performance, and market share are no longer the sole measure of an organization's success. Spiritual values such as integrity, compassion, and courage can be expressed at work in ways that sustain the financial requirements of the organization but also enrich the employee, the company, and the community through a greater good beyond the bottom line.

Many examples can be found of organizational heroes who have empowered their employees to express their spirit at work. Jeffrey Swartz, chief executive officer (CEO) of Timberland, encourages each of his 6,000 employees at the popular boot and clothing company to spend 1 week per year volunteering in their community at full pay. The legendary Aaron Feuerstein of Malden Mills, maker of Polartec fleece, kept his workers on payroll for months even though his plant had burned down and many employees had no place to work. However, you don't have to be a CEO to have significant meaningful impact on your workplace.

Although we can think of many ways to express spirituality at work, one perspective that we and our coauthors have developed and found to be impactful and simple is the framework we call "The Wisdom of Solomon at Work."[12] We identified six universal values that have withstood the test of time and continue to be relevant and important today:

- Wisdom
- Justice
- Integrity
- Compassion
- Courage
- Faith

The Wisdom of Solomon framework encourages us to identify how we express these spiritual values in our home and personal life and then to explore how we might bring these values to work. Rather than limiting our workplace behavior to the narrow perspectives of profit and performance, we can bring our spirit to work and operate with integrity regardless of the situations in which we find ourselves. As we have witnessed successful corporations wither under the shadow of insider trading, accounting fraud, and corrupt leadership, it is clear to us that the Wisdom of Solomon could have helped them follow a different path.

In sum, we suggest that by searching and finding your purpose, you will be able to better organize your life and thus experience the pinnacle of happiness and productivity. Purpose can serve as your daily guide. It can help you use all of your resources in the most effective manner to reach your ultimate potential. Purpose is an integral aspect of all effective self-leaders, so it can also help *you* attain peak performance in all aspects of your life. The following quotation from Dorothea Brande illustrates the importance of having purpose in your life.

> In the long run it makes little difference how cleverly others are deceived; if we are not doing what we are best equipped to do, or doing well what we have undertaken as our personal contribution to the world's work, at least by way of an earnestly followed avocation, there will be a core of unhappiness in our lives which will be more and more difficult to ignore as the years pass.

A checklist for using self-goal-setting follows. We also have provided an exercise that includes a guide for conducting an all-important self-analysis and an opportunity to establish your purpose and long- and short-term goals.

CHECKLIST FOR SELF-GOAL SETTING

Use self-goal setting to establish direction for your efforts.

- Conduct a self-analysis to help you establish your purpose and related long-term goals (see the self-goal–setting exercise).
- Establish long-term goals for your life and career—for example, what do you want to be doing and where do you want to be 10 years from now? In 20 years?

(continued)

- Establish short-term goals for your immediate efforts.
- Keep your goals specific and concrete.
- Make your goals challenging but reasonable for your abilities.
- When feasible, let others know about your goals to provide you with added incentive to achieve them.

SELF-GOAL–SETTING EXERCISE

Answer the following questions to help you establish your purpose and set your long- and short-term goals.

LONG-TERM GOALS

1. Who am I?
2. What am I meant to do?
3. What am I trying to do with my life?
4. What do I value most in life—for example, prestige, wealth, acceptance of others, family relations?
5. a. What would I most like to accomplish during my lifetime? (Note: An interesting way to approach this question is to write your ideal obituary including all that you would like to have accomplished before you die.)
   b. Develop a list of long-term goals.

GOALS FOR DEVELOPING ABILITIES TO REACH LONG-TERM GOALS

6. What are my primary strengths and weaknesses that are related to what I would like to accomplish?
7. What do I need to do to prepare myself to accomplish my long-term goals—for example, education, skills that need to be developed?

SHORT-TERM GOALS

8. What do I need to do now (today, this week) to progress toward my long-term goals—for example, read a book, complete a task? Develop a list of short-term goals and update it as needed.

Rudy! Rudy! Rudy!
Dreams Do Come True

A case in point of the benefits of goal-setting is Rudy Ruettiger, or Rudy. Effective self-leadership skills paid off for Rudy in the game of football and in the game of life.

While growing up, Rudy had a dream. His dream was to play football for Notre Dame University. However, on graduation from high school, with no money for college, he spent 4 years working in a power plant and as a Navy yeoman on a communications commandship. During this time, Rudy never lost sight of his important long-term goal. He applied to Notre Dame but was rejected. Did he quit? Did he complain about how unfair life was? No, he did not. After receiving the rejection, he drove in the middle of the night to Notre Dame. Upon his arrival, he met a priest who counseled him to enroll at Holy Cross, a community college within a stone's throw of Notre Dame. Although Holy Cross was not Notre Dame, Rudy viewed succeeding there as his short-term goal toward reaching his long-term goal of playing football for Notre Dame.

Thus Rudy, already in his early twenties, entered Holy Cross in 1972. During his first three terms at Holy Cross, Rudy reapplied for admission into Notre Dame but was rejected each time due to his poor academic record. However, Rudy never gave up. He buckled down and put his heart and energy into improving his grades. Although unwelcome as a student, he started working as a groundskeeper at Notre Dame Stadium and he boxed in campus charity fights. In 1974, Rudy applied once more for admittance into Notre Dame and was accepted. Once he was accepted, he told the head football coach, Ara Parseghian, that he would make the team. His fighting spirit and ability to take punishment from the larger players earned him a spot on the practice squad; he helped the team prepare for each week's game during practice sessions but sat in the stands during the games.

Rudy played on the practice squad for 2 years. As his second season neared its completion, the now 26-year-old Rudy had yet to play in a real game. The coach finally allowed him to suit up for the last game of the season and stand on the sidelines with the rest of the team. With 17 seconds remaining in the game and Notre Dame leading comfortably, his teammates and fans shouted, "Rudy, Rudy, Rudy!" Everyone wanted to see Rudy play. Even more, Rudy wanted to play and to finally live his dream. The coach got the message and put Rudy in the game. Was Rudy prepared for this opportunity? Indeed! In fact, he sacked the opponent's quarterback for a 5-yard loss. When the time ran out, his fellow teammates carried him off the field on their shoulders.

Rudy's actions relay what can happen to effective self-leaders. We, as self-leaders—who direct our own lives by setting long-term goals, who set short-term goals to achieve these bigger ideals, and who tirelessly persist toward making the goals happen—will enjoy personal excellence in life.

SOURCE: Adapted from C. P. Neck, "Rudy! Rudy! Rudy! Dreams Do Come True" in H. Sims and C. Manz, *Company of Heroes: Unleashing the Power of Self-Leadership* (New York: Wiley, 1996): 119–120.

Self-Reward

> After giving the speech she walked as though floating to her chair, sat down slowly, and thought to herself, "Well I'll be darned, I did a hell of a job."

One of the most powerful methods we possess to lead ourselves to new achievements is self-reward. We can influence our actions positively by rewarding ourselves for desirable behavior. Furthermore, we are capable of rewarding ourselves at a physical and a mental level.

At the physical level, we can reward ourselves with objects that we desire. In our executive development seminars and college courses, people have revealed numerous ways that they have used things they value to reward themselves. Some of the rewards they have used for completing tasks include ice cream, shopping, watching television, listening to a stereo, and going out to eat. By rewarding themselves with desired items such as these, they exert a positive effect on their future work activity. An example is a salesperson who enjoys the self-rewarding gift of a day off or an expensive dinner after making a big sale.

The important point is that we can reward ourselves with things that we enjoy when we accomplish desired objectives. Many of us do this without realizing it is happening. To increase our own motivation and effectiveness, the challenge is to identify those things we find rewarding and then use them systematically to reward our behavior. By having an exquisite dinner out after we finally talk to that problem employee we've been avoiding, we are providing incentive for ourselves to use similar desired behavior in the future.

We also can reward ourselves at a mental level. We can do this through internal speech and through our imagination. If a salesperson finally makes that big sale, he or she may be calm on the outside, but if we could listen inside we might hear, "Ya hoo . . . I did it . . . I'm a genius . . . I'm the best . . . Ya hoo . . ." We've often wondered what a professional baseball player is thinking after hitting the game-winning home run in the ninth inning. We all probably engage in self-rewarding internal speech after big successes like these, but why not try this powerful method for less momentous occasions? In fact, we probably could improve our own behavior significantly if we purposefully sought out our desirable behaviors and gave ourselves an internal word of praise.

This practice would be especially useful for those persons who are quick to criticize themselves. We have a choice between focusing on what we've done right and thus building ourselves up, and focusing on what we've done wrong and thus getting down on ourselves. The research done in this area indicates that the former strategy is more effective. Guilt and self-criticism may have their place in keeping us from engaging in socially and personally undesirable acts, but to rely on these mechanisms and ignore self-praise is a poor way to lead ourselves. Our self-esteem, enthusiasm, and enjoyment in life would likely suffer.

We also can reward ourselves in our imagination. For example, we can journey to our favorite vacation spot in an instant through our imagination. We can close our eyes and see the deep blue waters and the white sand beaches with seagulls overhead, and feel the warm sun on our face. Or maybe it's the cool air we feel rushing across our face as our skis glide gracefully through the pure white, new-fallen snow. Wherever and whatever the place, we can go there in an instant, and we can take the trip as a reward for finally getting that difficult report done or for accomplishing some other task. We might even hang a picture of the place on a wall and keep souvenirs nearby to help us make that mental trip when we choose to make it.

In fact, we can combine the physical and mental levels to exercise a particularly powerful self-reward strategy. We could take short, imaginary trips as we accomplish our tasks throughout the year and then physically enjoy our vacation after the months of hard work. By doing so we are rewarding our short-run and long-run activities. Also, the actual vacation will renew the basis for especially enjoyable imaginary trips when our mind is called on to reproduce the physical setting once we are back at work.

We also can use our imagination to reward ourselves in countless other ways. We can picture the success and esteem we will experience and enjoy when we finally get that promotion we are working toward. Enjoyment of such an image after completion of each difficult task can help us maintain the motivation we need as we face our labors. Indeed, the mind is capable of being a powerfully motivating tool. If we are to become truly effective self-leaders, we need to master the use of this tool. In doing so, we can make the effort we expend seem worthwhile if not truly enjoyable. A checklist to guide your attempts in mastering self-reward follows, with an exercise to help you put these steps into practice.

CHECKLIST FOR SELF-REWARD

Achieve self-motivation through self-reward.

- Identify what motivates you—which objects, thoughts, images.
- Identify your behaviors and activities that you believe are especially desirable.
- Reward yourself when you successfully complete an activity or engage in desirable behavior.
- Potential rewards you can use include:
    1. Desired physical objects such as an expensive dinner, a night out on the town, simply a cup of coffee or a snack, or reading a good book
    2. Enjoyable or praising thoughts such as thinking to yourself that you performed well and reminding yourself of future benefits you might receive from continued high performance
    3. Pleasant images such as imagination of your favorite vacation spot
- Develop the habit of being self-praising and self-rewarding for your accomplishments.

SELF-REWARD EXERCISE

Identify what you find rewarding.

1. What physical objects or events do you find rewarding—for example, a delicious dinner, an evening out?
2. What thoughts or images do you find rewarding—for example, self-praising thoughts, imagination of your favorite vacation spot, thoughts about future career success and prestige?
3. Identify behaviors that you would like to increase or improve upon that require special motivation for you to do them—for example, reading a technical book, working on a difficult project. Make a list.
4. Try rewarding yourself for working on the activities you have identified in step 3. Use physical and mental rewards. Keep track of your efforts on these behaviors, the rewards you use, and the results and ideas for future improvement—for example, more effective rewards discovered—stemming from the self-reward process.

Behavior	Rewards Used	Results and Ideas

Self-Punishment

> After giving the speech, she dragged herself to her chair, sat down deject-edly, and thought to herself, "I really did a lousy job."

One way that we lead ourselves is through the application of various self-punishments. Unfortunately, many individuals rely too heavily on this approach. Habitual guilt and self-criticism can impair motivation and creativity.

Self-punishment operates in much the same way as self-reward in that it focuses on self-applied consequences for behavior. The difference is that it involves negative rather than positive self-applied results to decrease undesired rather than increase desired behavior. A salesperson, for example, might engage in self-punishment after making (in his or her opinion) a poor sales presentation. Refusing to play that weekly game of golf or watching the big game on television and instead working endlessly on the sales presentation is an example of how self-punishment might be carried out at the physical level. At the mental level, negative internal speech ("I really did a lousy job . . . I should be ashamed of myself") or images of possible negative results of the behavior (imagining loss of one's job and not being able to afford to pay the bills and support the family) can provide the self-punishments.

Research and writing have generally indicated that self-punishment is not an effective strategy for controlling behavior. First, if we are applying the punishment to ourselves, we can freely avoid it. If we decide purposefully to use self-punishment to eliminate our undesired behaviors, we are likely to find that we will not use it consistently because it is unpleasant and we can choose to avoid it. Second, those who use it consistently (often in a habitual manner without realizing it) are likely to become discouraged and not enjoy their work.

At times, though, we need to work on our negative behaviors, so what can we do? Probably a better strategy would be to try to remove any rewards supporting the problem behavior and apply self-reward when we do things right. Self-observation will be important to accomplish this strategy. For example, imagine that we identify our problem behavior as watching too much television. One thing we might do is allow ourselves to watch only our second or third choice of programs on certain days, thus removing some of the reward of watching. Also, we could keep a record of how much television we are watching and reward ourselves when we substantially decrease our viewing time (for example, an expensive dinner out or even a free night of endless TV viewing).

Similar strategies could be used to deal with many of our problem behaviors. Self-punishment might be useful at times, such as when we experience guilt after doing something we know is obviously wrong. To live without a conscience would perhaps be the same as being in-human. In most cases, though, we can deal more constructively with our problem behaviors by studying them, removing the rewards that support them, and rewarding related behaviors that are desirable. The goal should be to take constructive action to correct these behaviors and not to demoralize and psychologically paralyze ourselves by dwelling on them.

A checklist for gaining control of your self-punishment patterns follows. An exercise also is provided to help you get started in constructively controlling your undesirable behaviors.

CHECKLIST FOR SELF-PUNISHMENT

Control your self-punishment patterns.

- Identify behaviors that create guilt.
- Identify your actions that result in self-critical feelings.
- Identify your destructive self-punitive tendencies.
- Work on reducing or eliminating habitual, destructive patterns of self-punishment.
- Try alternative strategies to self-punishment for dealing with your negative behavior, such as the following:
  - Identify and remove rewards that support your negative behavior.
  - Establish rewards for behaviors that are more desirable than your negative behaviors and that could be substituted for them.
- In general, reserve self-punishment for only your very wrong, seriously negative behaviors.

SELF-PUNISHMENT EXERCISE

Study your self-punishment patterns.

1. What are some of the behaviors that result in feelings of guilt?
2. What are some of the behaviors that result in your feeling critical about yourself?
3. Think about the behaviors that you have identified in step 1 and step 2. Is your guilt and self-criticism constructive or destructive?
4. In the next few days, try a different self-leadership strategy for dealing with your undesirable behavior in cases when you think your self-punishment is destructive.
   a. Try to identify and remove rewards that are encouraging your negative behaviors.
   b. Try reinforcing related, more desirable behaviors—for example, rewarding yourself for being calm and dealing rationally with conflicts with others rather than exploding with anger.

Keep track of your progress.

Undesirable Behavior	Strategy Used	Comments

Practice

"Hey, isn't this the third time you've been out here hitting balls this week?"

"Yes, it is. I'm tired of playing golf in the wrong fairway. I'm going to practice until I get rid of this slice."

One way we can improve our behavior is through practice. This point is stated clearly by Muhammad Ali, former world heavyweight boxing champion and Olympic gold medalist, as he remarked:

The fight is won or lost far away from witnesses—behind the lines, in the gym, and out there on the road, long before I dance under those lights.

Indeed, by going over activities before we are called on to perform them when it counts, we can detect problems and make corrections. In doing so, we avoid costly errors. For example, suppose we have developed a work plan for our place of employment that we strongly believe will improve profits for the company and working conditions for workers. Also, suppose we have been allowed 15 minutes to propose the plan to a group of executives who will decide whether it is to be adopted. We will want to make those 15 minutes count, so it is in our best interest to practice the presentation ahead of time.

Practice can be at a physical and a mental level. For the situation just discussed, we can verbally practice our presentation in front of a mirror or in front of willing friends, or we can go over the key points we want to make in our minds. Olympic athletes can take the same approach: They can practice their events repeatedly at a physical level as well as rehearse them mentally before competing.

Also, practice can be paired with self-rewards to increase motivation and self-confidence. In addition to mentally rehearsing our presentation, for example, we can picture praise from our audience and adoption of the plan. An Olympic athlete could picture winning the gold medal and the benefits that go with such an accomplishment.

Practice can be a powerful strategy to improve our behavior. The challenge is to apply it systematically. In essence, we need to practice practicing. The key is to develop the ability to identify the important parts of a given task, to practice them physically and mentally, and to pair our practices with rewards. The more important the activity is, the more important it is to practice. Practice might not make perfect, but it can make better—if we do it.

A checklist for practice follows. An exercise also is provided to get you started practicing.

CHECKLIST FOR PRACTICE

Improve future performance through practice.

- Identify especially important upcoming challenges.
- Note the important components of these future challenges.
- Physically practice these key components—for example, practice an important oral presentation, focusing special effort on the key points to be made.
- Mentally practice key components while thinking about possible improvements in the performance plan.
- Pair your practice with rewards—for example, while mentally going over a future challenge, imagine a positive, rewarding outcome resulting from your actions.

PRACTICE EXERCISE

Use physical and mental practice to improve your performance. Make notes.

1. Identify those challenges you believe will be most important for you in the next few weeks.

2. What are the important components or steps involved in dealing with the challenges identified in step 1?

3. Practice your performance plan to deal with these challenges. Practice physically and mentally, and pair your practice with rewards. Keep a record of your practices and possible improvements and ideas identified during them.

Behavior Practiced   When Practiced   Ideas and Possible Improvements

Over the past few years, we have asked hundreds of participants in our executive development seminars and university classes to complete personal improvement projects applying the strategies that are presented in this book. They were simply asked to apply the strategies that seemed most appealing to them to address some aspect of their work or life that they would like to improve. The following short case (and the ones at the end of chapters 4 and 6) is a composite based on the experiences of these managers, executives, college students, doctors, technical specialists, and persons on many other career paths.

The Case of the Sales Rep Who Neglected to Bring in New Clients

Jack was a district sales representative for AB Company. He was highly regarded by his clients. He serviced his accounts about as well as anyone in the business. Jack developed good relationships with these clients by continuously looking for new and better ways to provide excellent service. He called on each and every client on a regular basis, and asked about their current needs and their inputs concerning suggestions for improving his service to them. Jack generally liked his customers and enjoyed talking and visiting with them.

Despite his strong commitment to service and the high level of satisfaction of his clients, Jack was considered only an average producer in the company. He rarely lost an existing account, but his success in bringing in new clients was low. He was selling in a

growing industry, and district sales representatives in his company were increasing their client base at a rate of about 9 percent per year. Jack, on the other hand, was increasing his clients by about 4 percent per year. The zone sales manager had just reviewed Jack's performance with him the day before and made it clear to Jack that his new customer growth was simply inadequate. Jack still felt a little angry as he recounted the conversation in his mind. After all, he did have the lowest rate of lost clients in his region, and a recent survey of his customers revealed a satisfaction level that was among the highest in the company.

Nevertheless, Jack realized that he was going to have to make some changes if he wanted to advance in the company. He was going to have to build his client base at an increased rate. At the same time, he realized that he simply did not enjoy calling on potentially new clients nearly as much as he did clients that he had gotten to know over the years and in many cases had developed personal friendships with.

To address the problem, Jack reasoned that he had to get a better handle on how he was spending his current time and efforts. He began by keeping a detailed log of his activities for a week (self-observation). He recorded the times that he undertook various tasks, what specifically he did, the purpose of the activity, and how long he spent on it. During this initial self-observation period, Jack made no effort to change his work routine. At the end of the observation period, he discovered some revealing patterns. First, he had spent about 47 hours (about 95 percent of his time) either doing routine paperwork, attending meetings, or servicing clients. He had spent less than a total of 2 hours on efforts to communicate with only three potential new clients, all of whom came from referrals from existing clients. Although he recognized the positive role of the referrals from satisfied customers (and he had received preliminary agreement for a modest sale to one of these referrals), Jack also realized that he was spending too little time on generating new business.

As a second step, Jack decided to set a goal to increase his time spent on seeking new customers to 6 hours over the next week and decided that he would further increase the time he spent on this activity by 0.5 hour per week over the next 4 weeks until he reached a total of 8 hours per week (self-goal-setting). After recording this goal on a pad of paper, Jack realized that he felt a bit uneasy about spending that much time on an activity he did not enjoy much. Furthermore, he knew his referrals would cover only a small portion of that time and he would have to spend much of the time proactively seeking new leads and making some cold calls on potential customers. He

concluded that he needed to create a way of rewarding himself for reaching his goal. His approach was to take a short coffee break immediately after each solid hour he spent on generating new business (self-reward). He also decided that if he met his goal, he would take his wife out to one of their favorite restaurants at the end of the week to celebrate. He also planned to add additional rewards for meeting his increasing goals over the coming weeks.

As an additional strategy, Jack hung a sign in front of his desk that read "Your best customers will be the ones you haven't even met yet" (cueing strategy). This helped Jack to keep his new goal constantly in mind and to feel positive about the possibility that many of the new clients he would gain could lead to some of his most satisfying relationships in the future. Finally, he spent some time in the office and at home rehearsing (practicing) new approaches for calling on potential new clients. He did this in front of a mirror, with his wife, or with a willing coworker. Interestingly, he discovered that when he rehearsed with others, they often gave him suggestions and tips on how to improve his approach.

Jack's self-leadership efforts proved successful. Over the next several weeks, he increased his goal to 10 hours per week spent on generating new business, which he faithfully met. In addition, he increased his generation of new clients to about 14 percent for the year, which was one of the highest levels in the region. He also was pleased to discover that his service to existing clients didn't suffer; he simply spent more time dedicated to the important needs of his customers. His performance review for the next year went well, and Jack received a substantial pay increase. Over time, Jack realized that he was good at generating new business. Although he didn't enjoy this activity as much as servicing existing clients, he was confident, with the aid of his self-leadership strategies, that he would be able to maintain significant success in this area for years to come.

This chapter has presented several strategies for understanding and improving self-leadership in the face of difficult challenges and activities. Checklists and exercises were provided to help make these ideas more concrete in terms of your own behavior. Hopefully you decided to take the time and exert the effort to try some of these exercises. The next chapter focuses on a different aspect of self-leadership, capitalizing on the "natural" rewards that come from performing attractive activities. ∎

Notes

1. An interesting book on this subject is by Carl E. Thoresen and Michael J. Mahoney, *Behavioral Self-Control* (New York: Holt, Rinehart and Winston, 1974).

2. See, for example, C. P. Neck and C. C. Manz, "Total Leadership Quality: Integrating Employee Self-Leadership and Total Quality Management" in D. Fedor and S. Ghosh (eds.), *Advances in the Management of Organization Quality*, vol. 1 (Greenwich, England: JAI Press, 1996): 39–77; and Michael J. Mahoney and Diane B. Arnkoff, "Self Management: Theory, Research, and Application" in J. P. Brady and D. Pomerleau (eds.), *Behavioral Medicine: Theory and Practice* (New York: John Wiley, 1979); and Charles C. Manz and Henry P. Sims, Jr., "Self-Management as a Substitute for Leadership: A Social Learning Theory Perspective," *Academy of Management Review* 5 (1980): 361–367. See also chapter 4 in Charles C. Manz and Henry P. Sims, Jr., *The New SuperLeadership: Leading Others to Lead Themselves* (San Francisco: Berrett-Koehler Publishers, Inc., 2001).

3. Merrill E. Douglas, *ABC Time Tips* (New York: McGraw-Hill, 1998).

4. *The Random House Dictionary* (New York: Random House, 1980): 376.

5. Richard J. Leider, *The Power of Purpose: Creating Meaning in Your Life and Work* (San Francisco: Berrett-Koehler Publishers, Inc., 1997): 1.

6. Leider, 2.

7. Leider, 1.

8. Viktor Frankel, *Man's Search for Meaning* (New York: Washington Square Press, 1984): 165.

9. Dan Townsend, *King Arthur and the Holy Grail* (Dandolf Productions, 1996). Taken from the Internet site excalibur.simplenet.com/ dandolf/Arthur%20%26%20the%20Grail.

10. John Matthews, *The Grail Tradition* (Rockport, MA: Element, Inc., 1990): 6.

11. See the Web site www.spiritatwork.com for a good overview of conferences, books and articles, meetings, courses, and research in the area of spirituality and work life.

12. See the book *The Wisdom of Solomon at Work: Ancient Virtues for Living and Leading Today* by Charles C. Manz, Karen P. Manz, Robert D. Marx, and Christopher P. Neck. (San Francisco: Berrett-Koehler Publishers, 2001).

CHAPTER

Scenic Views, Sunshine, and the Joys of Traveling

or Creating the Self-Motivating Situation

We need to stop looking at work as simply a means of earning a living and start realizing it is one of the elemental ingredients of making a life.

—LUCI SWINDOLL

One morning a national leader gazed in the mirror and knew his time had passed. He decided that he should select his successor. He believed this to be his most important remaining decision. Under his guidance, his tribe had grown from a small, disorganized, self-defeating people into a powerful nation with much pride and sense of purpose.

So it was that he summoned his two greatest governors to his quarters—one of whom he would choose as his successor. He turned to the first governor, whose accomplishments were great though significantly less than those of the other, and said, "Tell me of your philosophy of leadership and of how you have accomplished what you have."

The first governor responded quickly and simply, "I have learned the skill of getting my people to do what they should do whether they like it or not."

Then the national leader put the question to the second governor, whose physical stature and manner were considerably less impressive but who for some reason had accomplished significantly more.

The second governor had to think for a few moments and then answered in a manner that was not so clear and simple. "I'm not really a leader at all," he began.

The great national leader was concerned with this response and was beginning to think that the first governor was a more likely choice.

"There are your leaders," the second governor continued as he motioned to the crowds of citizens outside the building.

Now the great leader was more thoughtful and curious about the second governor's response though still unsure of its merit. All was quiet for some time, and the great leader motioned to the crowd and asked, "Then what is the secret of their leadership?"

The second governor again responded slowly and thoughtfully. "They believe in what they are doing and for the most part enjoy doing it. You see, the secret to leading oneself is doing what one believes is worthwhile and doing so specifically because you believe in it and enjoy doing it. I'm just a coordinator of sorts. I simply try to help them discover what it is that they see as worthwhile and the capability, interest, and desire within them to do it. I find if I can help them get themselves pointed in the same purposeful, exciting direction, there is an unleashing of a tremendous power for progress."

Now the great leader thought awhile concerning the second governor's response with a sense of awe and wonder. "I have made my decision," he stated after a few moments.

All those inside and outside the chamber within hearing distance grew very silent straining to listen.

"For the future leadership of our nation, I have chosen these people!" he proclaimed while motioning with both hands to the crowds outside. And then turning to the second governor he said, "And you shall coordinate them."

This chapter is concerned with a naturally positive approach to self-leadership. The approach reminds me of a statement that a childhood doctor made frequently: In response to a statement such as "Doctor, it hurts when I do this," he would say, "Then don't do that." This chapter is concerned with a principle involving similar logic but that has a reversed focus. That is, if you say, "I like to do that," the parallel self-leadership response would be, "Then do it." Please don't misinterpret this discussion as a "do your own thing no matter what" message. Indeed, restrictions to this approach such as laws, your own values, and so on must be addressed. The primary purpose of this chapter, however, is to get across one simple idea: the desirability of using the natural rewards (your naturally motivating activities and tasks) toward the pursuit of more effective self-leadership. Hopefully, reading this book is shaping up to be this type of naturally rewarding activity as opposed to a "getting yourself to do a dreaded, unattractive but necessary" type of task.

Take a few moments to assess your own tendencies regarding the use of natural rewards. Select the number in the questionnaire shown in Table 4-1 that best describes your position in response to statements 1 through 15. These statements might seem similar to those in Chapter 3 — but respond to each one. Follow the directions provided for scoring your responses.

Interpreting Your Score

Your score for A through E suggests your current self-leadership tendencies concerning several self-leadership strategies that will be addressed in this chapter. Your score for each of these strategies could range from 3 (a total absence of the strategy in your

TABLE 4-1   Self-Leadership Questionnaire 2 (SLQ2)
Self-Assessment Questionnaire for Creating the Self-Motivating Situation

	Describes Me Very Well	Describes Me Well	Describes Me Somewhat	Does Not Describe Me Very Well	Does Not Describe Me At All
1. I try to be aware of what activities in my work I especially enjoy.	5	4	3	2	1
2. When I have a choice, I try to do my work in places (a comfortable room, outdoors, etc.) that I like.	5	4	3	2	1
3. I seek out activities in my work that I enjoy doing.	5	4	3	2	1
4. I spend more time thinking about the good things rather then the drawbacks of my job.	5	4	3	2	1
5. I pay more attention to enjoyment of my work itself rather than rewards I will receive for doing it.	5	4	3	2	1
6. I know the parts of my job that I really like doing.	5	4	3	2	1
7. I try to arrange to do my work in pleasant surroundings when possible.	5	4	3	2	1
8. When I have a choice, I try to do my work in ways that I enjoy rather than just trying to get it over with.	5	4	3	2	1
9. While I work, I think less about things I don't like about my job than things I like.	5	4	3	2	1
10. My thinking focuses more on the things I like about actually doing my work than on benefits I expect to receive.	5	4	3	2	1
11. I can name the things I do in my job that I really enjoy.	5	4	3	2	1
12. When I can, I do my work in surroundings that I like.	5	4	3	2	1
13. I try to build activities into my work that I like doing.	5	4	3	2	1
14. I focus my thinking on the pleasant rather than on the unpleasant feelings I have about my job.	5	4	3	2	1
15. I think less about the rewards I expect to receive for doing my job than on the enjoyment of actually doing it.	5	4	3	2	1

TABLE 4-1   (Continued)

Directions for scoring. Add the numbers you circled for each statement as indicated below to determine your score for each self-leadership strategy.

		Scores
A.	Distinguishing natural rewards (add your responses for 1, 6, and 11)	_____
B.	Choosing pleasant surroundings (add your responses for 2, 7, and 12)	_____
C.	Building naturally rewarding activities into your work (add your responses for 3, 8, and 13)	_____
D.	Focusing on the pleasant aspects in your work (add your responses for 4, 9, and 14)	_____
E.	Focusing on natural rewards rather than external rewards (add your responses for 5, 10, and 15)	_____
X.	Total score (add the scores for A through E)	_____

---

current self-leadership) to 15 (a very high level of the strategy in your current self-leadership). Your score on A through E can be interpreted as follows:

1. A score of 3 or 4 indicates a *very low* level of the strategy.

2. A score of 5 to 7 indicates a *low* level of the strategy.

3. A score of 8 to 10 indicates a *moderate* level of the strategy.

4. A score of 11 to 13 indicates a *high* level of the strategy.

5. A score of 14 or 15 indicates a *very high* level of the strategy.

Each of these strategies addressed by the questionnaire should generally contribute to personal performance and effectiveness. Therefore, a high score on A through E suggests a high level of self-leadership, which offers potential to enhance performance. Each of the specific strategies is discussed in more detail throughout the remainder of the chapter.

Your score on X indicates your overall use of the self-leadership strategies and could range from a low of 15 to a high of 75. Your score on X can be interpreted as follows:

1. A score of 15 to 22 indicates a *very low* overall level of the strategies.

2. A score of 23 to 37 indicates a *low* overall level of the strategies.

3. A score of 38 to 52 indicates a *moderate* overall level of the strategies.

4. A score of 53 to 67 indicates a *high* overall level of the strategies.

5. A score of 68 to 75 indicates a *very high* overall level of the strategies.

In general, a high score on X suggests that you possess some positive self-leadership tendencies. Your score on the questionnaire reflects what you believe are your current self-leadership tendencies. Regardless of your score, the remainder of this chapter is designed to help you implement and improve upon several self-leadership strategies. This chapter will provide you with a basis for better understanding and more effectively using the power of natural rewards.

THE NATURAL REWARDS

An important distinction has been emphasized in the psychology literature between two basic types of rewards.[1] One type of reward is the externally administered reward we most often identify regarding work organizations. A list of examples of this type of reward would include praise, a pay raise, time off, a promotion, an award of some kind, a bonus, and so on. In the previous chapter, it was argued that many such rewards can be self-applied to influence positively our own motivation.

A second type of reward also can be identified that is generally less recognized and less understood but that is no less important. This second type concerns rewards that are so closely tied to a given task or activity that the two cannot be separated. For example, an individual who enjoys reading the newspaper and spends a great deal of time doing so is engaging in an activity that could be described as naturally rewarding. No special externally administered or self-administered incentives are necessary to motivate this behavior. The incentives are built into the task itself. Of course, some externally applied rewards might result, such as compliments from others on being well informed. This emphasizes the fact that both types of rewards can be and often are at work at the same time. Still, the importance and power of these natural rewards should be recognized and, where possible, positively used.

In Chapter 2, it was suggested that an Olympic athlete could use many strategies to help motivate the difficult training behavior that accompanies success. It also was suggested that some of the necessary training might be naturally enjoyable—such as the natural enjoyment of pole vaulting for a decathlon athlete. This chapter is intended to suggest ways of harnessing the power of these naturally rewarding activities. It is designed to help us do what we want to do (and to like it) on our journey toward becoming what we choose for our lives.

WHAT MAKES ACTIVITIES NATURALLY REWARDING?

Two primary features can be identified as being descriptive of naturally rewarding activities: (1) They tend to make us feel more *competent* and (2) they tend to help us feel *self-controlling* (or self-determining).[2] In addition, another aspect of naturally rewarding activities will be suggested, which concerns the sense of *purpose* we derive from them. The following discussion will address each of these features separately.

Feelings of Competence

One common aspect of naturally rewarding activities is that they frequently make us feel more competent. We often enjoy tasks that we perform well. People who perform well in a sport often like that sport; persons who do well in school often like school.

If we think of activities we especially like, we probably will find that many or most of them contribute to our feelings of competence in some way. For example, persons often enjoy talking about their work, hobbies, or some other area in which they possess knowledge and skill. If we find that a conversation we're having with another person is lagging, we might begin asking about his or her work or hobbies—a probable result is an increase of interest and enjoyment of the discussion for that person. It can be argued that talking about a person's area of expertise contributes to that person's feelings of competence and is therefore naturally rewarding. Perhaps you have noticed increased interest on your own part when you have talked to others about your skill areas. Similarly, as we improve our performance in an activity, we often find it becomes more enjoyable. A couple of good shots on the golf course, for example, can go a long way toward enticing us to play again in the future.

Activities that tend to make us feel more competent are often tied to external rewards of some kind. Compliments from others on our display of knowledge in a conversation, and "oohs" and "aahs" for spectacular shots on the golf course, will motivate us to continue these activities. The focus here, however, is on the naturally rewarding aspects of the activity itself. The feeling of strength and power for a runner who is in good condition can contribute to feelings of competence and be rewarding in itself, apart from trophies won and praise received for effort. The same logic applies to our activities in general.

Feelings of Self-Control

A second common characteristic of naturally enjoyable activities is that they frequently make us feel more self-controlling. Humans seem to have a natural tendency to want to control their own destinies. From toddlers whose favorite activities seem to be the off-limits "no-no's" to adults who dream of being their own boss and independently wealthy, the desire for personal control as opposed to external control is readily apparent.

We tend to want to be a major force in determining what happens around us. For example, most of us would prefer to make important decisions that directly affect us, such as where we will live, where we will work, whom we will marry, and so forth, rather than to have someone else dictate these things to us. In a more general sense, we prefer to control aspects of our world rather than have them control us. Those of us who have been in situations where our every move seemed to be dictated by someone else, some rule or regulation, or some other external source know the helpless feelings of a lack of self-control. Conversely, projects, hobbies, or other activities that we choose to undertake and in which we choose the method by which they will be performed contribute to our feelings of self-determination.

The combination of our desire for feelings of competence and self-control often results in a pattern in our behavior. This pattern involves a search for challenges that we are capable of overcoming and then expending effort to overcome them. Increasing our running distance by an extra half mile, cutting a stroke off our golf game, or striving to achieve a reasonable increase in our performance rating at work all potentially reflect this kind of pattern. Grappling with reasonable challenges can be naturally rewarding because overcoming them can contribute to our feelings of competence and self-control. Activities that accomplish this result are probably prime candidates to try to increase or build into our tasks to make them more enjoyable. In essence, we use the potential effects of different activities on our feelings of competence and self-control as a guide for helping us select the features to build into our tasks, or to focus our thoughts on while performing them, to make our effort more naturally rewarding. These features often take the form of a personal challenge of some sort that we are capable of overcoming.

Feelings of Purpose

One more important feature of naturally rewarding activities needs to be considered. This feature involves providing us with a sense of purpose. Even if a task makes us feel more competent and more self-controlling, we still might have a difficult time naturally enjoying and being motivated by it if we do not believe in its worthiness. As discussed, most of us yearn for purpose and meaning. The troubling emergence of what has been frequently referred to as a mid-life crisis in many persons accents this idea. When looking back on one's life and looking ahead to the future, we have a basic need to feel that what we are doing is of value. The best vacuum cleaner salesperson in the world (who is obviously competent and who has freely chosen the profession, and is otherwise self-determining) still might not enjoy the work if he or she has no self-confidence about the job. From where, then, do these feelings of purpose and meaning emerge?

One aspect of naturally rewarding activities, which many would argue provides a sense of purpose, involves helping or expressing goodwill toward others. The term *altruism* often is used in connection with this idea. The author Hans Seyle has suggested that the way to enjoy a rewarding lifestyle, free of disabling stress, is to practice "altruistic egoism."[3] In essence, this idea involves helping others and "earning their love" while at the same time recognizing one's own needs and enhancing oneself (egoism). Seyle explains that the natural biological nature of humankind drives people toward self-preservation, or what might be described more bluntly as *selfishness*. The philosophy suggests that only by marrying this innate, self-centered nature with an attitude of winning the goodwill and respect of others through altruistic efforts will a happy, meaningful life result. On the other hand, in a scholarly article analyzing evidence from biology and psychology, another author, Martin Hoffman, concludes that an altruistic motive might exist in humans apart from egoistic motives.[4] The evidence suggests that altruism might be a part of human nature that is not entwined with any selfish motive.

Regardless of why altruism can potentially add purpose to a task or, more generally, to one's life, it should not be overlooked. It could be the key to achieving feelings of purpose and meaning. We might never fully understand the altruistic urge, let alone human nature, but the essence of purpose might be centered in the simple idea of helping our fellow humans (and possibly *ourselves* in the process).

We can identify many pursuits that provide people with a feeling of purpose and that at least appear to exist apart from altruistic motives. A scientist whose life purpose is encompassed in advancement of pure scientific knowledge exemplifies this idea, but then doesn't advancement of science potentially serve an altruistic end—the betterment of all people? Whether scientists are significantly motivated by this aspect of their work may vary from person to person. The challenge is for each of us to search inside ourselves to find what provides us with a feeling of purpose. Altruism might well be at the heart of this search for most of us.

> The true destiny of man[kind] is to find his [or her] true destiny, and only then to obtain peace.

A checklist for guiding attempts to discover the natural rewards in your life follows. An exercise is provided to help you get started in identifying your natural rewards.

CHECKLIST FOR DISCOVERING YOUR NATURAL REWARDS

Discover your natural rewards.

- Identify tasks or activities that you naturally enjoy—in which the rewards for doing them are built into, rather than separate from, the tasks themselves.
- To help you find these naturally rewarding tasks, look for activities that:
  - Help make you feel competent
  - Help make you feel self-controlling
  - Provide you with a sense of purpose

DISCOVERING YOUR NATURAL REWARDS EXERCISE

Discover your naturally rewarding tasks. Make notes.

1. List some of the activities that you naturally enjoy doing—when the incentive for doing these activities is built into the tasks rather than being separate from the tasks.
2. Classify the above activities, and expand your list by identifying activities that provide you with a sense of:
   a. Competence
   b. Self-control
   c. Purpose
3. Identify activities that accomplish all three (provide you with a sense of competence, self-control, and purpose). Note that activities that do not accomplish all three might not be true naturally rewarding activities.

TAPPING THE POWER OF NATURAL REWARDS

Two primary approaches to using natural rewards to enhance our self-leadership will be discussed here. These are (1) building more naturally enjoyable features into our life's activities, and (2) intentionally focusing our thoughts on the naturally rewarding aspects of our activities.

Building Natural Rewards into Our Life's Activities

The blizzard hit the forest with a tremendous force, leaving a deep layer of new-fallen snow. The beaver was in a bad mood as he struggled toward the river. The snow made it hard to move, and he was irritable as he trudged along. Then the beaver noticed the whistling of the otter, who was sliding and rolling playfully over slopes on his way to the river. "Why are you whistling on this horrible day?" snapped the beaver, obviously irritated. "Why, it's a great day," the otter sang out, "the best day I've had since yesterday—which was great, too." The beaver sneered at this response and continued to complain as he trudged forward. The otter continued to slide and roll along playfully, whistling while he went. They both reached the river.

The logic of the first approach to using natural rewards in exercising self-leadership involves identifying aspects of our endeavors that we naturally enjoy and trying to increase these as much as is reasonably possible. For example, a business meeting can be held in an appealing location. The same matters addressed in a formal conference room of an office building will take on a different flavor when they are addressed in a relaxed meeting room at a beautiful resort. Similarly, persons who like direct conversations with fellow employees can enjoy communicating a message face to face if they choose rather than struggling to write a formal memo. The point is that we usually can identify several ways to accomplish many of our activities. By choosing to accomplish these tasks in more enjoyable ways, we are building in natural rewards for our efforts.

Let us illustrate these ideas further with the example of a person who runs or jogs regularly. This individual might run to obtain benefits such as increased endurance and strength, weight control, reduced stress, or the like. The individual might, on the other hand, run for the sheer enjoyment of the activity. We know an individual who has been a runner for many years—he takes his running seriously enough to play at it. Though he has trained hard and performed well in organized races, including marathons, he does not understand those who run as a chosen form of leisure or exercise in a dull and monotonous way. A person who runs around a track day after day, probably through some force of will to get in shape, exemplifies this dull approach.

Natural rewards can be built into the activity to make it more enjoyable and more naturally rewarding if a runner chooses. One way to do this is to run in enjoyable places. Running along an ocean shore while listening to the peaceful rhythm of powerful white-crested waves and watching graceful seagulls overhead can be an exhilarating experience. Alternatively, a person could run on a forest trail while listening to the singing of birds and the rushing of streams, and perhaps see an occasional squirrel, deer, or other wildlife. The running could be done in the early morning or at dusk while enjoying a brightly colored horizon. Running can be a more enjoyable experience for those runners who choose to make it so.

The emphasis up to this point has been on the more obvious aspects of making activities more naturally enjoyable, that is, by choosing a pleasant context for the task, which is, in essence, part of the task. Another focus involves following the guidelines suggested earlier: We can search for features of our activities that provide us with a feeling of competence, self-control, and purpose, which are prime factors for making a task more naturally rewarding. For a runner, this might involve undertaking a reasonable challenge, such as a slightly longer run than usual over challenging terrain. The task is all the better if it provides the runner with a sense of purpose because of a belief that he or she is setting a positive example and being an inspiration for others or the run is part of a fund-raising drive for charity, for example.

Similarly, our work and lives can be more naturally rewarding if we take them seriously enough to play at them and make them more enjoyable. One of my (Charles Manz) first experiences in my academic career was at a conference I attended shortly after I began my doctoral studies. I was excited about the opportunity to listen to some of the most esteemed and respected faculty from across the country. At one of the first meetings of this gathering, doctoral students from dozens of universities (myself included) listened to perhaps the foremost scholar at the meeting present a rather bleak message: We (the listening students) would never again have as light a workload as we had at that time. We were told by the speaker—and his comments were later supported by other speakers—that we should be prepared for long and demanding work hours (perhaps 50, 60, 70, 80, or more hours per week) in our future careers. The listening students, many of whom already felt overworked, were obviously less than enthusiastic about this crystal-ball view of their futures. Although some of the rewarding aspects of our profession were discussed, the underlying message seemed to be that if we really want to be successful, we should be prepared to work our tails off.

I have thought back to that experience many times. I was impressed with the speakers and believe they were competent people. For this reason, I am all the more disturbed by the message conveyed and the effect it had on the audience. Our (both C. Manz and C. Neck) problem with the philosophy presented (one that we believe is all too common) was that it suggested that the path to successful careers and the ultimate achievement of our life's goals is an agonizing, uphill climb. We do agree that sacrifices and intense effort are often integral parts of achieving one's goals (hence, the considerable value of self-discipline-oriented self-leadership strategies such as those presented in the last chapter). Our underlying philosophy concerning achievement and success, however, is different.

In essence, we would argue that the road to success, although often rocky and challenging, should be made as naturally rewarding as possible. To the extent that a person pursues worthwhile challenges that are naturally enjoyed, a built-in motivation is established. We can explore our present work and life for the activities we enjoy that help us make progress toward our goals. We can build enjoyment into our work. We can plan our careers so that we enjoyably progress toward our desired destinies.

Although we believe the accredited speakers at the meeting would agree with much of this logic, their message conveyed, intentionally or unintentionally, a less pleasant view of work. Here's a better message.

> Fellow students of that meeting, don't work your tails off. Instead, work as little as possible, for when you are doing what you naturally enjoy, work is no longer work. As Confucius said, "Find a job you love and you will never have to work another day in your life." If you enjoy what you do, it will not seem like work. Expend the effort and put in the necessary hours, but build in natural rewards and work on what you believe in, in the way you most enjoy. When possible, take part in worthwhile activities that you naturally like. Self-leadership strategies (such as those presented in the last chapter) can help us overcome our formidable obstacles when they arise, but when we have a choice, we should use the power of natural rewards. We can truly reach the pinnacle of success (and create a better world in the process) if our work is inspired.

Furthermore, making your work more enjoyable can provide benefits beyond your work success. Did you know that when you can say, "I love my work," you reduce your risk of heart disease? In fact, a study completed by the Massachusetts Department of Health, Education, and Welfare investigated the cause of heart disease. Participants were asked two questions: "Are you happy?" and "Do you love your work?" The results suggest that those who answered yes have a better chance of not getting heart disease.[5]

Majestic Moments: An Exercise to Help You Discover Naturally Rewarding Work

This exercise involves a difficult mental climb to the peak of your own personal mountain. This self-discovery climb will involve a journey toward helping you identify qualities that make you unique—that make you a special human being.

Taking the First Step

This first step requires taking an inventory of your life's experiences. Specifically, contemplate the years of your life. Consider the times in your life that involved a "majestic moment" (MM). These are the times when you felt an ultimate flow of

(continued)

all your energies; when you enjoyed a sense of accomplishment, exhilaration, happiness, and self-pride; and/or when you felt that this was the purpose of your life and where you belonged. Further, these were the times when you really stretched yourself—making full use of your abilities. Your MM could be related to work, school, a sport, a hobby, or anything in which you played a meaningful role. It is important to note that your MM does not have to be a majestic moment for someone else. Your majestic moments are defined by you alone. What some-one else thinks is not important. Finally, try to think of an MM that is majestic not because you won something or finished first (focuses on an outcome), but rather one that is majestic because of the actual task (process) it involved.

List four of your majestic moments.

1. ____

2. ____

3. ____

4. ____

You have just completed the first part of your journey.
Remember that the longest journey begins with the first step.

Second Step: The Climb

Think about the events in step 1 in detail. Recall the experience as vividly as pos-sible. Try to picture the details of the experience. What were your feelings and thoughts? Mentally relive the experience.

Note several aspects of your majestic moments using the following cues.

1. What skills did you utilize while achieving your MM (physical, mental, writing, speak-ing, helping, nurturing, etc.)?

2. What were the conditions that surrounded or led to your MM (activity was important, challenging, high autonomy, high accountability, involved teamwork, etc.)?

Third Step: Enjoy the View

Recall the quote by Confucius given earlier in the chapter. Wouldn't it be won-derful to have a majestic moment every day of your life—every time that you performed your job? If you select a job that allows you to utilize the skills you observed in step 2 and/or involves the surrounding conditions you noted, chances are good that you will experience MMs during performance of your job and, thus, truly enjoy what you do.

Are you currently employed in a job that you don't find enjoyable? Are you majoring in something that you won't enjoy working at upon graduation? If you answered yes to either of these questions, then try to identify a position in your organization or in another field that would utilize your MM skills and that would match your MM environment. Another approach is to find ways in your current job to use your MM abilities and change the environment to resemble more closely the MM environment identified in this exercise. It might not be easy to find a new job or alter your current one to fit these MM criteria, but if you persevere it can happen. If you are determined, then you can find a job that doesn't seem like work.

By working on what you believe (by living your purpose) and by building natural rewards into your job to make it more enjoyable, your health and performance could improve greatly.

Would you like to experience more enjoyment and natural rewards while performing your job? If so, the following checklist and exercise should help you find a job (or alter your current one) that is filled with natural, rewarding activities.

CHECKLIST FOR BUILDING NATURAL REWARDS INTO YOUR ACTIVITIES

Build natural rewards into your tasks.

- Examine the nature of your current activities.
- Identify pleasing contexts (places) in which you could perform your work to make it more pleasant and naturally rewarding.
- Identify activities that could be built into your tasks (different ways of accomplishing the same things) that make your work naturally rewarding (that provide you with a sense of competence, self-control, and purpose).
- Redesign your tasks by working in the contexts and building in the activities that make them more naturally enjoyable.

BUILDING NATURAL REWARDS INTO YOUR ACTIVITIES EXERCISE

Follow these steps. Make notes.

1. List some tasks you need to do that you do not particularly enjoy doing.
2. Try to identify different, more pleasant contexts in which you could perform these tasks.
3. Identify activities you find naturally rewarding that could possibly be built into the tasks (that provide you with a sense of competence, self-control, and purpose). Refer to the list that you developed in the "discovering your natural rewards exercise" as a starting point, and identify additional activities.
4. Redesign your tasks. Use your ideas from step 2 and step 3 as a basis for redesigning some of your tasks. Specify plans for redesigning tasks, including contexts and activities that could make your work more naturally rewarding.

Focusing on the Natural Rewards

The three men were called crafters and worked side by side using the same tools and crafting the same items. The first man thought the sun was too hot, his tools were too old, and that his arms got too tired. He frowned and grumbled as he worked. The second man thought of the money he would receive on payday, the praise that would be bestowed upon him for his good work, and of being promoted to chief crafter one day. He did not think about his work much at all—only of his better future ahead. The third man thought of the pure, clean air that fed his lungs, of the feeling of power and strength he enjoyed as he worked his tools, and of the admiration he felt for the finely shaped item he was creating with his own hands. He smiled, for he was not working at all.

A second approach to tapping the power of natural rewards centers on the focus of our thoughts while we perform tasks. We can choose to think about, talk about, and, in general, focus on the parts of our work that we don't like—and thereby feel badly about our work. We also can choose to direct our focus on the rewards we expect to receive from performing our labor (money, praise, recognition) and thus be motivated by our images of the future. On the other hand, we can choose to direct our focus on the naturally enjoyable aspects of our work and enjoy the activity for its immediate value. It will be argued here that this latter focus is the key to naturally enjoying our present endeavors.

Most of our activities possess what we would consider pleasant and unpleasant characteristics. A runner, for example, can think about heat and sweat, sore muscles, exhaustion, blisters, and a score of other things most people would consider unpleasant; or a runner can think about praise from others for his or her excellent physical condition, of a potentially longer life due to improved health, and the feeling of power and strength that accompanies a conditioned runner's stride. Both types of thoughts are available to a runner, and the type the runner chooses will significantly affect his or her enjoyment of the activity.

FOCUSING ON PLEASANT VERSUS UNPLEASANT FEATURES OF OUR TASKS EXERCISE

Follow the steps provided. Note that the logic of this exercise is simple—the power of which can be experienced only by trying it. It is important that you take the time and exert the effort to try it out.

1. Identify and list several aspects of your work under the following two categories.
   ASPECTS OF MY WORK
   Pleasant   Unpleasant

2. Later, when you're at work, focus your thoughts on the pleasant features you have identified. You might even try focusing your conversations with others on these features. Then switch your focus to the unpleasant features while you work.

3. Comment on the results of this exercise. How did you feel while you focused your thoughts on the pleasant aspects of your work? The unpleasant features? How did your focus affect your motivation and satisfaction with your work?

This simple logic can be applied to our major activities in life. If we th moment about the various aspects of our work, we probably can identify several p ant and unpleasant features. To bring these ideas to life, try the preceding exercise.

This exercise, though perhaps sounding overly simplistic, emphasizes a crucial aspect of the importance of choice in self-leadership. Perhaps the most critical aspect of self-leadership concerns the way we choose to think about our tasks. The importance of our thinking patterns is considered in more detail in the remainder of this chapter and in Chapters 5 and 6. Suffice it to say here that if we believe we have freedom to choose our thoughts (if we do not possess freedom in our thoughts, it would seem that we possess no freedom at all), then choosing to focus on the pleasant aspects of our work, rather than on the unpleasant, appears to be a logical strategy for helping us experience natural enjoyment.

Another issue that should be addressed centers on the question, "Does it make any difference what pleasant features of our activities we focus upon?" The position taken here is that it does. Recall that we can distinguish between rewards that are separable from a task and natural rewards that are built into a task and that largely derive from effects on our feelings of competence, self-determination, and purpose. By focusing on the former type of reward, our incentive for doing the task comes from the expectation of future rewards. By focusing on the latter, our reason for doing the task is the task itself. This latter focus is the key to natural enjoyment of our work. These ideas suggest another simple exercise that follows.

If you are not able to identify naturally rewarding activities such as those suggested in the exercise, you are probably either in the wrong job or you are not sincerely trying to identify them. Focusing on rewards that are separate from the work should lead to motivation based on future expected benefits. Focusing on rewards that are part of the work should result in an enhanced enjoyment of your present activities for their own sake.

FOCUSING ON DIFFERENT TYPES OF REWARDS EXERCISE

1. List the rewarding aspects of your work under the following two categories. In the first category, list things such as monetary incentives (salary and bonuses), praise and recognition received from superiors and fellow workers, possible promotion, awards, and so on. In the second category, list things that are part of performing the work such as feelings of skill you experience while working, enjoyable interactions with people who help you accomplish tasks, fascinating learning that accompanies your performances, overcoming challenges, and so on.

   REWARDING ASPECTS OF MY WORK

   Separate from the work   Part of the work

2. While at work, focus your thoughts on the rewards listed under the category "Separate from the work" for a while, and then focus on rewards that are listed under the category "Part of the work."

3. Comment on the results of this exercise. How did you feel while you focused on rewards that are separate from the work? Part of the work? How did your focus affect your motivation concerning your present efforts? Your future efforts? Your enjoyment of the task itself?

ggested, then, is not only to focus our thoughts on the rewarding
, but further, to be selective in our focus on the kinds of rewards.
e indicates that when external rewards are increased for work that
workers might be motivated subsequently by the rewards rather than
ient of the task.[6] It might be that people reevaluate their reasons for
ole work when external rewards are emphasized. Receiving the rewards
quently take precedence over natural enjoyment of the activities. Although
oint has been controversial among researchers, a fairly substantial body of
e, nas been accumulated to support it. The significance of this viewpoint for the
presen. discussion is that focusing our thoughts on expected external rewards could
undermine our immediate enjoyment of the task. Although such a focus might be useful
for some tasks that do not possess many naturally enjoyable qualities, focusing on natural rewards is preferable because it optimizes the enjoyment of our present activities.

The following checklist helps guide efforts toward achieving motivation through
focusing on the natural rewards. Take a moment to look over this checklist and to reflect
on how you can take advantage of the power of natural rewards in your future activities.

CHECKLIST FOR FOCUSING ON THE NATURAL REWARDS

Focus your thoughts on the natural rewards.

- Identify the pleasant, enjoyable aspects of your tasks.
- Distinguish between the rewarding aspects of your work that are separable from the work itself, and those rewarding aspects that are part of (built into) your work.
- Focus your thoughts on the pleasant rather than on the unpleasant aspects of your tasks while you work.
- When possible, focus your thoughts on the rewards that are part of (not separate from) the actual task to obtain motivation and satisfaction for your immediate efforts.
- Work toward developing the ability and habit of distinguishing and focusing on the natural rewards in your work.

(NOTE: The intention of this strategy is not to ignore our problems and concerns. Important negative issues regarding our work must be considered. Although we exert effort, focusing our thoughts on the naturally rewarding aspects of our tasks can provide motivational and emotional benefits, including those occasions when we must deal with problems and concerns that are part of the job.)

Knowledge Self-Leadership: Coping with Business Environments of the Twenty-First Century

—Paul D. Tiedt and Vikas Anand

"How do you do it? You must be reading up and learning new stuff all the time. Where do you get the time?" Mike asked Jill Moore as they stepped out of their meeting. Mike and Jill were members of their organi-

zation's strategic planning cell. Mike was commenting on the fact that whenever Jill was asked to address a problem or examine an alternative, she invariably had it well researched and analyzed at the next meeting; in fact, whatever the issue Jill typically made a thorough and well-researched presentation and confidently tackled most queries that arose during the meeting. "Actually, I don't think I spend more time than anyone else," said Jill. "The people who work with me are extremely knowledgeable; and I depend on them and other folks I know."

Today's business environments often have been referred to as "knowledge environments." We need to gather and analyze large amounts of information for even simple decisions in organizations. Yet information is increasingly dispersed and is subject to rapid obsolescence. To cope with such environments, we need to display "knowledge self-leadership," a means ensuring that we have required knowledge when we need it. This approach should be considered an integral part of self-leadership. When we don't possess needed knowledge, we will be unable to develop the feeling of competence so essential to building natural rewards in our tasks.

A few years ago, knowledge self-leadership would have involved educating and training ourselves in order to develop our expertise. Unfortunately, this approach is not sufficient to help us in today's environments. Apart from the fact that the amount of required knowledge is much larger than ever before, we cannot determine in advance the specific skills and information needed in the future. Consequently, to cope with today's knowledge environments, we need to adopt an approach that involves supplementing our personal knowledge with external knowledge—the knowledge that we can obtain on demand from other individuals.

We should view ourselves as part of a knowledge network that comprises our peers, subordinates, and colleagues. Knowledge self-leadership should be seen as an approach that expands this knowledge network and makes us more efficient at seeking information from it. This approach comprises four steps. First, we should be *willing to seek knowledge* from this network when the occasion arises. This also implies that when other individuals in the network acquire new skills, the knowledge potentially available to us is expanded. Thus, apart from augmenting our own knowledge base, a knowledge self-leadership approach also requires us to encourage people around us to become more knowledgeable.

Second, a knowledge self-leadership approach requires us to *invest in building relationships* and social networks. It is extremely unlikely that we will possess reliable and accurate knowledge that is relevant to the numerous decisions that we encounter in organizations (or for that matter, even in our day-to-day life). The wider our knowledge network is the more likely it is that we will encounter someone with the required expertise or information. We can develop these relationships by making extra efforts to get to know our coworkers, as well as other individuals who work with our customers or our suppliers. In addition, we need to

(continued)

make added efforts to recognize the specific expertise of each person so that we have complete information about our knowledge network. This, in turn, will allow us to tap the network more efficiently.

Third, we need to *motivate* people in our knowledge network to share their knowledge with us when we need it. In order to do this, we need to share our knowledge and information with other individuals at their time of need. Doing so creates a bond and motivates people in our knowledge network to help us when we need it. This is especially important because we often are tempted to hoard knowledge in order to make ourselves feel indispensable; however, hoarding knowledge can be extremely counterproductive from a knowledge self-management perspective. Additionally, we must make efforts to provide credit to those who shared their knowledge with us. Even a simple action such as a note of appreciation to knowledge givers acts as a reward that motivates them to repeat their actions in the future.

Finally, developing our knowledge network is not a substitute for *augmenting our personal knowledge*. Rather, it should be treated as a supplement, and we should continuously focus on learning efforts that increase our personal knowledge. Becoming more knowledgeable in our areas of expertise increases our attractiveness to other members in our knowledge network and increases the probability that we will receive desired information when needed. Further, continuously increasing our personal knowledge base increases our ability to use knowledge provided by members of our knowledge network. For example, if we have a nuclear scientist in our knowledge network, we cannot hope to use that person's knowledge without some basic understanding of physics.

Knowledge self-leadership can significantly expand the knowledge and information available to us when we make critical decisions. By adopting the behaviors described, we can get a head start in coping with the increasing information and knowledge demands of the twenty-first century.

SOURCE: This article draws on the following published articles: Anand, V., W. H. Glick, & C. C. Manz. (2002). Thriving on the Knowledge of Outsiders: Tapping Organizational Social Capital. *Academy of Management Executive* 16(1): 87–101; Anand, V., C. C. Manz, & W. H. Glick. (1998). An Organizational Memory Approach to Information Management. *Academy of Management Review* 23(4): 796–809.

A CLOSING COMMENT

Before leaving this chapter, we comment about the relationship, and perhaps the seeming contradictions, between the ideas of the present chapter and Chapter 3. The present chapter has emphasized natural rewards built into a task, whereas Chapter 3 suggested several self-applied techniques, including the use of self-applied rewards that are separable from the task. Both approaches were presented as ways to achieve more effective self-leadership. The strategies of the two chapters can complement each other well. Strategies such as those presented in Chapter 3 can be used in especially difficult situations that are lacking in natural rewards. The intention is to maintain the self-leadership necessary to work through the difficult and unattractive but necessary tasks on the way to activities and future job positions that we can naturally enjoy. In the meantime, an effort should be made to build in and focus on the natural rewards that are available. To the extent that this can be accomplished, greater enjoyment of our present moments can be obtained.

Consider the following case. It was developed from some of the experiences of participants in our training programs and courses (e.g., managers, executives, and MBA students) who applied the kinds of strategies presented in this chapter.</P></BM>

The Case of the External Rewards That Were Just Not Enough

Anne was a staff manager in a large American corporation. She had a generally strong track record and was known to be a hard worker who completed her assignments on time. She was not considered especially creative or innovative, but she was dependable. In performing her job, Anne relied heavily on the directions and cues she received from her boss, the department manager, Bob Jones. The past performance reviews Anne received from Bob were strong but not outstanding.

This was the occasion of Anne's third performance review since she had joined the department. As Anne looked over the review form Bob had just handed her, she couldn't help thinking that it looked familiar. This feeling was soon confirmed. "As you probably realize, Anne, your performance rating this year is essentially the same as last year," Bob stated. "Once again, you have turned in a strong performance and you are showing steady progress in your department. I think any recommendation for promotion is still a ways off, but keep up your hard work and dependability and you'll get there eventually."

Anne felt pretty satisfied with the way the review had gone and with the overall evaluation she had received. But when Bob asked, "Is there anything else you'd like to talk about?" she decided to raise an issue that was troubling her.

"Bob, there is one thing that is bothering me."

"What's that, Anne?"

"Well, I seem to be losing interest in my job. I'm not sure that I'm motivated by it anymore. At first I was challenged by it and was anxious to perform my best. Now I'm not so sure I like what I'm doing. I'm just not sure I'm having much fun anymore."

A surprised look came over Bob's face. He hadn't expected any response to his final question, and now he kind of regretted that he had asked it at all. "Do you have any suggestions or ideas on how to deal with the problem?" Bob asked in a voice that sounded a little confused and unsure.

Anne paused for a moment but then decided to say what she was thinking. "Well, I've been doing some reading, and I ran across an article that suggested that we should redesign our own jobs. The main idea is to change what we do and how we do it so that it better fits our strengths and interests while still meeting our responsibilities. I've been thinking about this for a few days now, and I've decided I'd like to try it if it's OK with you. You see, at first it was enough to follow your directions and to receive your approval when I got a job done. Now I'd like to contribute more of my creativity and innovative abilities, and tailor my job to fit me a little better."

Bob was a bit unsure of all that Anne was saying, but he could tell she felt strongly about these ideas. Because she had always been a dependable employee, he agreed to let her try this new strategy, although he wasn't sure what to expect.

Over the next few weeks, a significant change came over Anne. At first she was a bit cautious about making changes and initiating things more on her own, but gradually she started coming up with new ideas. She developed a new computerized tracking system for organizing the department's work projects (she liked working on computers). She also created a weekly report form that she used to keep Bob informed of her progress on specific projects. This weekly report took the place of her daily multiple visits to Bob's office to seek his guidance. She found that these kinds of accomplishments gave her a feeling of increased competence in her work, and checking in with Bob less often gave her a sense of having more control over her own activities. Also, as Anne saw her new computer tracking system being used by other people in the department (and some even followed her example in using the weekly progress report form), she felt an increased sense of purpose because of the benefits she was providing for others.

Over time, Anne became known as one of the most creative and enthusiastic employees in the division. When her next performance review rolled around, Anne looked with satisfaction at the review form Bob handed to her on which she was rated as an outstanding performer and recommended for a promotion. As she scanned

the form, a puzzled look came over her face. "Did you make a mistake in identifying my job position?" she asked Bob.

"No, not really, Anne. In my book you are no longer a staff administrator. You are an advanced project manager. I made a special request for this job title change and a raise in grade for you. That's partly why you're getting this big raise," Bob said with a smile as he leaned over and showed her the sizable pay increase she was to receive recorded on a sheet of paper. You see, I've recommended you for a more significant promotion, but in the meantime you've already been promoted."

Anne beamed as she took in all this good news. Then she stopped and got a serious look on her face. "You know, Bob, thinking back over what has happened in the past year, the thing I value most is how I feel about my work. I was kind of confused when we met a year ago. I wanted to like my job more for its own value. Now I really like what I do. Thanks for the pay raise and title change, but I've got to be honest." She paused and looked him right in the eye for emphasis. "I'd probably be excited about the coming year even if you had given me a minimal raise and didn't recommend that I be promoted. I've designed a job that fits me, that I'm good at, that I enjoy, and through which I can make contributions that benefit others. I can't wait to see what I can accomplish this year."

The inspirational writer Norman Vincent Peale, who has been read by and has affected the thinking and living of millions of people, made a statement in one of his books that parallels the major thrust of this chapter closely. He said, "Do your job naturally, because you like it, and success will take care of itself."[7] If we practice a self-leadership style that allows us natural enjoyment of our activities, we can indeed derive the motivation we need to be successful—especially at enjoying life. ■

Notes

1. See Edward Deci, *Intrinsic Motivation* (New York: Plenum, 1975).

2. See, for example, *ibid.;* and Edward Deci and Richard Ryan, "The Empirical Exploration of Intrinsic Motivational Processes" in L. Berkowitz (ed.), *Advances in Experimental Social Psychology* 13 (1980).

3. Hans Seyle, *Stress Without Distress* (New York: Signet Books, 1974).

4. Martin L. Hoffman, "Is Altruism Part of Human Nature?" *Journal of Personality and Social Psychology* 40 (1981): 121–137.

5. Deepak Chopra, *Magical Mind, Magical Body* (Niles, IL: Nightingale Conant Corp., 1991).

6. See, for example, Deci, *Intrinsic Motivation*; and Edward Deci, John Nezlek, and Louise Sheinman, "Characteristics of the Rewarder and Intrinsic Motivation of the Rewardee," *Journal of Personality and Social Psychology* 40 (1981): 1–10.

7. Norman Vincent Peale, *A Guide to Confident Living* (Greenwich, CT: Fawcett Crest Books, 1948): 59.

CHAPTER 5

Travel Thinking

or Redesigning Our Psychological Worlds

The mind is its own place, and in itself can make a Heaven of Hell,
a Hell of Heaven.

—JOHN MILTON

The traveler physically collapsed and groaned with relief as he gazed upon the white-haired old man who sat before him. He paused for a moment to cautiously look over the sheer cliff he had just climbed to reach the top of the mountain. He gazed upon the thick jungle beyond that had been his home for many days. "Old man," he gasped, "I have traveled for days to speak to you because many have said you are among the wisest of all the living. I must know the true nature of life—is it good or is it bad?"

The white-haired old man responded with a question of his own. "Tell me first—how do you see life, my son?"

The traveler looked away, frowning, and said slowly and sadly, "I believe life is bad—people are selfish and basically cruel, and fate always seems anxious to deliver a disheartening blow." Then he turned to the old man and asked, with obvious anguish in his voice, "Is this the nature of life?"

"Yes," responded the old man, "This is the nature of life, my son."

The traveler dropped his gaze, his face going blank, pulled himself to his feet, and solemnly began his descent back down the cliff.

A few moments later another traveler pulled himself up over the edge of the cliff and collapsed at the feet of the white-haired old man. "Tell me, old man of much wisdom," he gasped, "What is the nature of life? Is it good or is it bad?"

The old man again asked the question, "Tell me first—how do you see life, my son?"

At this question the traveler looked hopefully into the old man's eyes. "Life can be hard, and the way is often difficult," he started, "but I believe the nature of life is basically good. People are not perfect, but I see much value in the heart of each I meet—even those that would be called the most lowly. I believe life is challenge and growth, and offers a sweet victory for those who try and endure. Is this the nature of life?" he asked as he continued his hopeful stare into the old man's eyes.

"Yes," responded the old man, "This is the nature of life, my son."

The emphasis of this chapter and the next one is on our unique psychological worlds. The viewpoint taken is that each of us experiences a uniquely different psychological world, even when faced with the same physical situations, because of the way we think. Our senses (sight, hearing, feeling, tasting, smelling, and perhaps other more mystical senses) are constantly bombarded with stimuli. Right this minute you are likely to have a potentially overwhelming number of things to focus on. What sights and what sounds are available to you, both near and distant? By the way, how do the bottoms of your feet feel? Are they tired, sore, comfortable? What kinds of things have you thought about lately? Have you spent more mental energy thinking about your problems or your opportunities?

The point is that we usually have a choice regarding what we focus on and what we think about. We can't deal with every possible stimulus that we come in contact with, nor can we deal with every possible thought. Of course, we don't have much of a choice about some of our thoughts, such as those we experience when struck by unexpected physical pain, but we *do* have a choice regarding what we think about much of the time. In addition, the things we choose to think about can be thought of in different ways. That is what this chapter and the next one are all about: what we choose to think about and how we choose to think about it. This might sound a little silly, but it is probably the most important part of self-leadership.

This chapter and Chapter 6 are thus devoted to providing a foundation for increasing your understanding of and improving your psychological world. Several strategies will be suggested that provide a basis for developing more desirable patterns of thought through which you see and deal with the world.

OUR PSYCHOLOGICAL WORLDS

What we experience in life is unique. No one else in the world can experience exactly what we do. We create our own psychological worlds by selecting what enters our minds (where the essence of human experience takes place) and what shape it takes after it does. The content of our unique psychological worlds determines the way we behave, and our behavior helps determine the nature of our physical worlds. All of these things together determine our progress toward our personal destinies. These ideas are represented pictorially in Figure 5-1.

We carry in our minds a world that is more real to us than the physical one within which we live. A cold winter blizzard has a different meaning to an avid skier than it does to an avid golfer. Identical physical conditions can result in joyful exultation for one person and depression and gloom for another. In fact, we are capable of turning potentially joyful, motivating situations into those of demoralizing gloom through our thoughts and resulting actions. For example, if we are invited to a social gathering of some kind, we can experience the event as an unhappy one by being overly self-conscious about our appearance and what we say. In essence, we would be choosing to focus our mind on negative

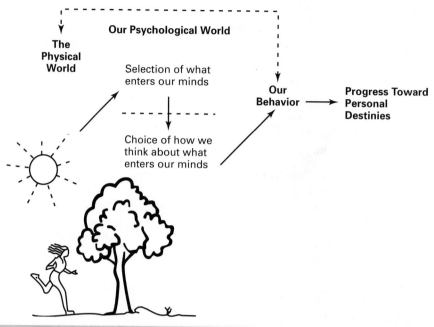

FIGURE 5-1 The Role of Our Psychological Worlds

aspects of a potentially positive situation. In general, we can look for the positive or negative in people and situations, and as a result create the psychological atmosphere in which we live and experience life. The following story should reinforce this point.

The Vision

Do you have a grand idea
To which some might laugh and smile?
They think it can't be done;
They call it a "someday I'll."

Then consider this story of two men;
Their business was selling shoes.
They were confronted with the same situation,
But each had differing views.

Both were sent to a far-away island
To test if their abilities were elite.
And they discovered, upon arrival,
The natives had nothing on their feet.

The first sadly called his boss
With a very large case of despair,
Relayed that there was no hope for business
Because everyone's feet were bare.

The second was filled with much elation;
Told his superior the good news.
Said he was going to make a million.
No one *yet* was wearing shoes.

The meaning in these few words
Is your thoughts can help you advance
Because to what some might spell disaster
Could be for you, your one big chance.

The secret to creating opportunities
Isn't money or political pull.
Simply, it's your attitude—
Is the glass half-empty or half-full?

A different real world example
Might help reveal this story's key.
It's a lesson of a pollinating insect,
The plight of the bumble bee.

According to the laws of science,
The bee should not be able to fly.
But this creature didn't acknowledge this
And instead gave flight a try.

So remember what history reveals
As you pinpoint your dreams with precision;
The primary keys to greatness
Are your attitude and your vision.

SOURCE: Christopher P. Neck, *Medicine for the Mind: Healing Words to Help You Soar* (New York: McGraw-Hill, 1996).

Because our actions help shape the physical world where we live, our psychological worlds ultimately have an impact on the physical world itself. In fact, the way we think about the physical world can be self-fulfilling. If we attend a social gathering worrying that we will not be accepted or liked by those present, we can make this fear come true. By being withdrawn and closed to others, these others are likely to reciprocate with similar behavior.

The remainder of this chapter and the next one will address different ways of analyzing and dealing with the way we think and how this affects our own self-leadership. The intention is to increase our understanding of and ability to deal with our psychological worlds. We can change our psychological worlds and our resulting behavior and experiences if we choose to do so. This viewpoint is consistent with psychological perspectives that place the responsibility for our actions and self-improvement where it belongs: on ourselves.[1] If we wish to achieve effective self-leadership and obtain personal effectiveness, we need to take responsibility for what we think and do. This approach is in direct contrast to the common tendency to place the responsibility for our actions on external sources such as authority figures or traumatic experiences from our childhoods. The focus is on dealing with and improving our immediate thinking and behavior rather than looking for reasons (excuses) for why we can't become what we wish to and are capable of becoming.

IS THERE POWER IN POSITIVE THINKING?

In the 1950s, the concept of more effective living was written about and read by many persons. This viewpoint, which can be called *positive thinking,* was introduced by the Reverend Norman Vincent Peale. Several books were published, including the well-known best-seller *The Power of Positive Thinking.*[2] Dr. Peale subsequently reported numerous cases in which persons overcame challenges and obstacles with the aid of positive thinking in support of his ideas.[3] Peale's work, however, was never subjected to what authorities in the area of psychology and human behavior would describe as scientific research. In fact, until recently, most academics in these areas would likely have considered his work with some amusement. Nevertheless, the effects of his work gained widespread public notoriety and attention such as few authors ever receive. More recently, evidence is accumulating in support of the many benefits to be gained from positive thinking.[4]

The idea of positive thinking is a useful reference point from which to consider improvement of our psychological worlds. Several different elements that offer the potential to help explain how our thinking can have an impact on our behavior and experience of life will be considered. These include our beliefs, our imagined experiences, our self-instruction (self-talk), and our thought patterns. The underlying logic is that if we make systematic efforts to change our thinking in beneficial ways, then we can improve our self-leadership. Beneficial thinking (or positive thinking, if you prefer) offers the potential to help us improve our personal effectiveness just as beneficial *behaving* does. In fact, as mentioned earlier, our behavior and our unique ways of thinking (mental behavior) are two primary, interrelated features in the total influence picture.

Self-Talk

Puff, puff, chug, chug, went the Little Blue Engine. "I think I can—I think I can—I think I can—I think I can—I."

Up, up, up. Faster and faster the little engine climbed, until at last they reached the top of the mountain.

And the Little Blue Engine smiled and seemed to say as she puffed steadily down the mountain, "I thought I could. I thought I could. I thought I could . . ."[5]

As children, many of us heard these words spoken by the Little Blue Engine, "I think I can, I think I can, I think I can . . ." These same words can benefit you today! This well-known phrase that was uttered by the Little Engine is an example of a mental strategy known as self-talk. The way in which the Little Blue Engine talked to itself clearly impacted its performance (getting over the mountain). In the same way, we believe that this mental technique known as self-talk (what you say to yourself) can help you perform better on the tasks that you are responsible for completing. In fact, if you are at this moment not doing well at school, on the job, or in your personal life, then it could possibly be related to what you are saying to yourself.

For example, consider for a moment if you have ever told yourself any of the following notions.

- It's going to be another one of those days!
- I don't have the talent.
- Jill (a roommate) just doesn't like me.
- I can't seem to get organized.
- It's going to be another blue Monday.
- I hate working within a team.
- If only I were a little smarter, then I could do this job well.
- If only I were taller.
- If only I had more time.
- If only I had more money.
- I'm too old to work that hard.
- I never get a break.
- I'll never be as good as the other students in class.
- Nothing ever seems to go right for me.
- Today just isn't my day.

If you are like most of us, you have told yourself negative things similar to these examples. These statements are negative in that they are "sappers." Sappers are types of self-talk that sap your energy, your self-confidence, and your happiness. Sappers are destructive self-talk; they prevent you from achieving your goals and feeling good about yourself. They serve as a self-fulfilling prophecy, because what you tell yourself every day usually ends up coming true. If you tell yourself that you won't have a good day, you won't. If you tell yourself that you can't lose weight, you can't. If you tell yourself that you won't enjoy your job, you won't. It is that simple.

The story of the Little Blue Engine's sister should reveal the impact of sapper self-talk on one's performance.

> Puff, puff, chug, chug, went the Little Blue Engine's twin sister. "I can't do this—I can't do this—The mountain is too big—I'm tired—I'm hungry—I'm irritable. This is impossible—I can't do this."
>
> Up, up, up. Slower, slower the little engine climbed until it just conked out.
>
> The Little Blue Engine's twin sister just frowned, and all depressed . . . she fell down the mountain. "I knew I couldn't do it—I knew I couldn't do it—I knew I couldn't do it."[6]

These stories represent the utilization of two different styles of the mental strategy self-talk—with two different outcomes. The Little Engine That Could used positive self-talk to make it over the huge mountain, and the children received their toys. The Little Engine's twin sister did not make it over the mountain because her negative self-talk sapped her energy and attitude. Rumor has it that the twin sister of the Little Engine (the Little Engine That Couldn't) is roaming around the country from train station to train station holding a sign that reads "I'll Work for Fuel."

These two train stories reveal the power that our self-talk can have on our success and happiness. As leading psychologist P. E. Butler writes:[7]

> We all talk to ourselves. What we say determines the direction and quality of our lives. Our self-talk can make the difference between happiness and despair, between self-confidence and self-doubt. Altering your self-talk may be the most important undertaking you will ever begin.

The life of Olympic decathlon gold medal winner Dan O'Brien serves as a real-world example of Butler's words. In 1992, O'Brien failed to even qualify for the U.S. Olympic team, despite being a favorite to win the gold medal. In the 1996 Olympic Games, he returned to win the gold medal that had alluded him 4 years earlier. So what was the difference for O'Brien between the 1992 Olympic Games and the 1996 Olympic Games? Why did he fail in 1992 and then crush the field in the decathlon events in 1996? Quite simply, O'Brien altered his self-talk. As O'Brien remarked:[8]

> Now I know what to do when I feel panic, when I'm nervous and get sick to my stomach . . . Instead of telling myself I'm tired and worn out, I say things like, My body is preparing for battle. This is how I'm supposed to feel.

For Dan O'Brien, changing his self-talk pushed him to Olympic glory. In the same way, changing your self-talk can enhance your life at work, school, home—everywhere.

The question you might be asking at the moment is How do I change my self-talk so that I can get over my own personal mountain to achieve my goals and dreams? The following exercise should help change your sapper self-talk to self-talk that can help you achieve maximum performance.

After answering these questions, take a close look at your responses. Do your self-talk examples contain a lot of destructive sappers, or is your self-talk supportive and motivating? If the former is true, then it is a signal to you that what you are telling yourself is causing many of the negative events, emotions, and so forth that you are experiencing within your life. In other words, you are the person responsible for sapping yourself.

The good news is now that you know you are talking to yourself in a negative way, you can change your self-talk. In the second part of this exercise, first write some of the negative self-talk that you were telling yourself (from the first part of the exercise). Then opposite this negative self-talk, write what you could have told yourself if you wanted your self-talk to be positive rather than sapping. We have provided several examples to help you.

DISCOVERING YOUR NEGATIVE SELF-TALK EXERCISE[9]

The following exercise will help you discover your negative self-talk during the course of a day. Please respond to the following questions. Each question will require a significant amount of thought. Fully relive the questions asked so that your answers are as accurate as possible.

1. List a project or activity that you have begun or considered beginning. What did you tell yourself as you started or failed to start it?

2. Think of a time when you were feeling lonely. What were you telling yourself at this time?

3. Think of a day when you were feeling stressed and overwhelmed at work. What were you telling yourself during this chaotic time?

4. What criticism have you recently faced from a coworker, fellow student, boss, or teacher? What were you telling yourself at this time and after the criticism?

5. Think of a recent compliment that a coworker, boss, teacher, or fellow student gave you. What were you saying to yourself at this time and after the compliment?

6. Think of a day when you were feeling negative about yourself. Once again, what were you saying to yourself at this time?

7. Think of a day when you were experiencing some symptoms of illness, such as a headache or achy bones. What were you telling yourself during the time when you were experiencing these symptoms?

NEGATIVE SELF-TALK

1. I hate working within a team.

2. I'll never lose this extra weight.

3. I'll never be able to earn a good grade on one of Dr. Neck's exams.

4. I am nervous about this job interview. I'm probably not as qualified as the other applicants.

5. She (he) will never go out with me. She (he) is out of my league. Why should I even bother asking her (him) on a date?

6. _____

7. _____

8. _____

POSITIVE SELF-TALK

1. Although this is a new experience for me, I know that if I make a good effort toward cooperating, we will make a much better product than if we were working by ourselves, and it will be fun getting to know each other.

2. I will lose this weight. It will take a lot of determination and willpower. I will achieve my goal of losing 1 pound per week.

3. Someone once said: "If you always do what you have always done, you will always get what you have always got." I need to find out what I'm doing wrong and correct my mistakes in terms of how I study and how I take tests. With effort and persistance, I will make an A on Dr. Neck's exam.

4. I am prepared for this interview. I have done my homework. This company needs my skills.

5. Seize the day! If I don't ask her (him) out, how will I ever know if she (he) would go out with me? Once she (he) gets to know me, she (he) will love me!

6. _____

7. _____

8. _____

Now examine the left-hand side of negative self-talk and the right-hand side of positive self-talk. Do you see a pattern? Do you see that the negative self-talk seems to be demotivating and negative, and it seems to sap energy, happiness, and self-confidence? Conversely, do you notice that the right-hand side of self-talk is positive, motivating, and supportive? Wouldn't you rather give yourself an advantage in all aspects of your life by making your self-talk positive in the future? Now that you are aware that your self-talk might be negative and have practiced changing it to be positive, you are well on your way.

Finally, you want to create the situation so that your positive self-talk becomes a habit for you. Try to be aware of what you are telling yourself over the next several weeks. From the moment you get up in the morning until the moment you go to sleep at night, remind yourself to talk positive. Repeat this exercise in this chapter daily, until you start to notice that you are having difficulty identifying any negative self-talk and have chased all the sappers away.

Beliefs

One of the greatest weight lifters of all time is the Russian Olympian Vasily Alexeev. Evidently he was trying to break a weight-lifting record of 500 pounds. He had lifted 499 pounds but couldn't for the life of him lift 500 pounds. Finally, his trainers put 501.5 pounds on his bar and rigged it so it looked like 499 pounds. Guess what happened? He lifted it easily. In fact, once he achieved this feat, other weight lifters went on to break his record. Why? Because they now knew it was possible to lift 500 pounds. Alexeev created a new mental outlook for weight lifters. Once people believed it was possible to lift 500 pounds, a major barrier to its accomplishment was removed.

The idea that what we believe is possible can be achieved is not new. The amazing fulfillment of many predictions made in books that have attempted to describe the future, such as *Future Shock, Brave New World,* and *1984,* suggests that what we believe can happen *can* happen.

One recent psychological perspective suggests that life problems tend to stem from dysfunctional thinking. In short, mental distortions form the basis for ineffective thinking that can hinder personal effectiveness and even lead to forms of depression. These distorted thoughts are based on some common dysfunctional beliefs that are activated by potentially troubling or disturbing situations. Based on the work of David Burns, we specify 11 primary categories of dysfunctional thinking.[10]

1. **Extreme thinking:** Things are seen as black or white (e.g., if total perfection is not achieved, then a perception of complete failure results).
2. **Overgeneralization:** A specific failure or negative result is generalized as an endless pattern.
3. **Mental filter:** A single negative detail is emphasized, thus distorting all other aspects of one's perception of reality.
4. **Disqualifying the positive:** Even if something positive is experienced, it is mentally disqualified from having any relevance or importance.
5. **Mind reading:** Drawing negative conclusions regarding situations despite a lack of concrete evidence to support these conclusions.
6. **Fortune-telling:** Arbitrarily predicting that things will turn out badly.

7. Magnifying and minimizing: Exaggerating the importance of negative factors and minimizing the importance of positive factors related to one's situation.

8. Emotional reasoning: Interpreting reality based on the negative emotions one experiences.

9. Should statements: Terms in one's self-talk such as "should" and "shouldn't" and "ought" and "must" are used to coerce or manipulate oneself into taking actions.

10. Labeling and mislabeling: Describing oneself, others, or an event with negative labels (e.g., "I'm a failure," "He is a cheat").

11. Personalization: Identifying oneself (blaming oneself) as the cause of negative events or outcomes that one is not primarily responsible for causing.

Burns argues that individuals need to confront these dysfunctional types of thinking and replace them with more rational thoughts (beliefs). For example, imagine an aspiring entrepreneur who freezes up during a business plan presentation to a venture capitalist (VC). The entrepreneur stumbles when asked about his valuation method even though he was an investment banker for 8 years. Additionally, the venture capitalist claims his pro forma statements are exaggerated given market conditions. Rather than defending his position, the entrepreneur agrees with the VC. The end result is zero financing from the venture capitalist. The entrepreneur leaves the presentation and thinks to himself, "I am the worst presenter. I'll never be able to get funding for this venture. Never."

This scenario presents an example of dysfunctional thinking based on the distorted belief of "extreme" thinking, which, as stated, refers to an individual's tendency to evaluate his or her personal situation in extreme black or white categories. The entrepreneur is not thinking that some of the most successful entrepreneurs present to more than 20 venture capitalists before receiving financing. He is evaluating his personal qualities in extreme black or white categories.

To alter this destructive belief, the entrepreneur must identify the dysfunction and then change the thoughts that occur to be more rational in nature. The entrepreneur could challenge thoughts of himself as a complete failure and revise his beliefs regarding himself by reversing his thoughts and thinking. "Some of the most successful entrepreneurs have to talk to close to two dozen venture capitalists before receiving financing. I shall learn from this mistake. It's not the end of the world; I will do better next time."[11]

An exercise for facilitating attempts at examining and improving your self-talk and beliefs follows.

AN EXERCISE IN THOUGHT MANAGEMENT

"You can't control the wind; but you can certainly adjust the sails"

1. Think of a recent time when you were feeling a negative emotion(s) (e.g., stress, anxiety, depression). List the negative emotion(s) you were experiencing.

2. What was the problem or task that you were facing at the time (e.g., job interview, relationship problem, test)?

3. List some of the things that you were telling yourself at this time.
   a.
   b.
   c.

(continued)

4. Regarding question 3, can you identify mental distortions (e.g., "extreme thinking") in your self-talk? If so, what are they?
   a.
   b.
   c.
   d.

5. How could you change (reword) your self-talk in question 3 to rid your internal speech of any mental distortions?
   a.
   b.
   c.

Notes

1. See, for example, Albert Ellis, *Better, Deeper, and More Enduring Brief Therapy: The Rational Emotive Behavior Therapy Approach* (New York: Brunner/Mazel, 1995); and Albert Ellis and John M. Whiteley (eds.), *Theoretical and Empirical Foundations of Rational Emotive Therapy* (Monterey, CA: Brooks/Cole, 1979).

2. Norman Vincent Peale, *The Power of Positive Thinking* (New York: Spire Books, 1956).

3. Norman Vincent Peale, *The Amazing Results of Positive Thinking* (New York: Fawcett Crest Books, 1959).

4. See, for example, Martin E. P. Seligman, *Learned Optimism* (New York: Pocket Books, 1998).

5. Watty Piper, *The Little Engine That Could* (New York: Platt & Munk, 1930).

6. From the article by C. P. Neck, H. M. Neck, and C. C. Manz, "Thought Self-Leadership: Mind Management for Entrepreneurs," *Journal of Developmental Entrepreneurship* 2 (1997): 25–36.

7. P. E. Butler, *Talking to Yourself: Learning the Language of Self-Support* (San Francisco: Harper and Row, 1981).

8. *USA Today,* "Sharpening Mental Skills," C3, 8 August 1996.

9. This exercise was adapted from a similar exercise in the book by C. Manz, C. P. Neck, J. Mancuso, and K. P. Manz, *For Team Members Only: Making Your Workplace Team Productive and Hassle-Free* (New York: AMACOM, 1997).

10. David Burns, *Feeling Good: The New Mood Therapy* (New York: Morrow, 1980).

11. For a more extensive discussion of mental self-leadership and entrepreneurship, see the article by C. P. Neck, H. M. Neck, and C. C. Manz, "Thought Self-Leadership: Mind Management for Entrepreneurs," *Journal of Developmental Entrepreneurship* 2 (1997): 25–36.

CHAPTER 6

Travel Thinking

Continued . . .

Every good thought you think is contributing its share
to the ultimate result of your life.

—GRENVILLE KLEISER

IMAGINED EXPERIENCE

Mary was gliding cautiously across the shimmering ice when one of her skates struck a hard lump on the otherwise smooth surface. Her weight shifted quickly forward, and she found herself flying through the air. She landed hard on her shoulder and right cheek, and felt pain go through her body. Her collarbone had been severely fractured, and she noticed blood trickling from a cut on her cheek. Then she heard a loud crack, and the ice began to separate underneath her. A moment later, she could scarcely breathe because of the icy cold water that enveloped her body. The extreme pain in her shoulder made it impossible for her to swim. She gulped water in an attempt to breathe. A desperate sense of panic swept over her, and . . .

"Mary are you going to put your skates on or do I have to do it for you?" asked Bill impatiently.

Mary stood up nervously, and turning to walk away said, "I don't think I want to learn to skate today; maybe some other time."

Would you believe us if we told you a technique is available that can help you perform better on the job? Would you believe us if we told you that this technique is available to you without spending a penny? The only cost to you is a relatively small amount of your time. In fact, this technique has been used by athletes for years to enhance their performance; golfers, basketball players, gymnasts, and ice-skaters use this technique to golf better, shoot better, tumble better, and skate better. The good news is that this technique is not only good for people participating in sports, but also for you as you work or go to school.

This technique is called *mental practice*. Mental practice involves imagining successful completion of an event before you physically complete the event. For example, consider an NBA basketball player who before a game pictures himself making all of his free throws. Because he has performed successfully in his mind, he should experience more confidence in the real-game situation and thus have a better chance at making his free throws.

Let's take another example involving two new salespersons about to make their first sales call. Suppose one salesperson experiences images of a muddled presentation that results in humiliating rejection from the client. This imagined experience could potentially block effective performance. In fact, such self-defeating images can promote corresponding negative results. The resulting lack of confidence and unconvincing presentation could lead to the failure that was imagined. Suppose the second salesperson imagines a positive experience resulting in a sizable sale and a worthwhile experience for both parties. In this case, the individual would likely possess a higher level of confidence going into the presentation and a higher probability of success.

The point is that we are capable of creating a unique world within ourselves. The essence of our experience of life is centered within the inner world we create. Many would agree that imagination of the pain and suffering we expect from a visit to the dentist is often, and perhaps usually, much worse than the actual event. The imagined negative experience could last for days prior to the actual appointment, which is over within minutes. Also, our imagined positive experiences can be more striking and powerful than their occurrence in the physical world. Anticipated events are often disappointing when they finally take place because they do not live up to our expectations. A party might not be as enjoyable as we imagined it would be, nor a vacation we planned for months. Films based on classic novels often fall short of the original work because the richness we can add to the book with our imaginations can rarely be achieved in visual form by filmmakers.

Symbolic, imagined experiences are an important component of the psychological worlds in which we interpret and experience life. If we can discover the effect they have on our lives, we can gain a better understanding of ourselves. We might find, for example, that before undertaking new challenges, we usually imagine negative results. To deal with this habitual negative thinking, we could intentionally imagine positive results before we take actions. Imagining a receptive, appreciative audience rather than a critical, hostile one before giving a speech, for example, might significantly help us overcome a fear of public speaking. By exercising greater choice and control over our imagined experiences, we can improve the quality of our psychological worlds and, potentially, our personal effectiveness.

To repeat, your mind is a powerful tool. You can use this tool to achieve great success. Just as a hammer serves no benefit if you don't know how to use it correctly, the "mental practice tool" only works if you know how to use it correctly. Following are steps to help you use this mind tool to enhance your performance. By using these steps repeatedly, you can enjoy the benefits of mental practice.

STEPS FOR SUCCESSFUL MENTAL PRACTICE

1. **Close your eyes.**
2. **Relax, concentrate, and focus.** Feel all the stress leaving your body. Start at your feet . . . feel all the stress leaving . . . go to your chest, then to the top of your head . . . feel all the stress leaving your body. Concentrate all of your energy on this mental practice exercise. Rid your mind of all distractions.

3. **Focus on a specific challenging situation** in which you would like mental practice to help you perform well.

4. **Talk positively to yourself.** Tell yourself several times that you are confident and that you have the power to perform well in this situation.

5. **Mentally picture yourself** right before you are to begin this task, event, project, and so forth.

6. Make sure to **stay concentrated, relaxed, and focused.**

7. Now **mentally rehearse** successful performance of this challenging situation several times. It is important that you see yourself in your mind as an active participant and not as a passive observer. For example, if you imagine that you are shooting a basketball during a game, make sure you are standing on the court shooting rather than watching yourself from the stands.

8. **Repeat step 7.**

9. **Open your eyes. Smile. Praise yourself.** You were successful in your mind. Now you should have a greater feeling of confidence that you will perform this event successfully in real situations.

The following are a few more tips to ensure that mental practice works for you.

- Make sure you visualize your actions in normal motion as opposed to slow motion.
- To help you relax (step 2), it might be helpful to mentally picture a calming scene such as a beach, a mountain, a forest, or a pond.
- Repetition of mental practice is critical—make sure you repeat these steps over and over to gain mental practice perfection.
- Space your practice sessions over several days rather than mentally practicing an event in one lengthy session.

A checklist also is provided to help you make improvements in your imagined experiences. A short exercise will help you get started making the changes that you see as desirable.

CHECKLIST FOR IMPROVING YOUR IMAGINED EXPERIENCE TENDENCIES

Use your imagination to facilitate desirable performance.

1. Analyze your current imagined experience tendencies. Ask yourself questions such as:
   - Do they focus on positive or negative outcomes of challenging tasks?
   - Do they generally facilitate or hinder my confidence and performance of tasks?
   - Are they realistic? Reasonable?

2. Identify destructive imagined experience tendencies such as the tendency to habitually and unrealistically imagine negative results for your actions.

3. Work to eliminate these destructive thought patterns by choosing to think about other things.

4. Purposefully choose to imagine sequences of events and outcomes that help clarify and motivate (rather than hinder) your efforts—for example, once you have chosen a course of action and are committed to it, motivate yourself by imagining positive rather than negative results of your efforts.

IMPROVING YOUR IMAGINED EXPERIENCE TENDENCIES EXERCISE

Follow the steps below.

1. Think about some recent challenges you have faced that especially provoked your imagination regarding the different actions you could take and the likely consequences of these different actions. Also, check yourself throughout the next few days as you face new challenges such as these.

2. Explore the nature of your imagined experiences on these occasions. Are they realistic? Do they tend to focus on the positive or the negative? Are they constructive?

3. Analyze the specific instances you identified in step 1 regarding the effect your imagination is having on your performance. What effect is your imagination having on your decisions (such as your willingness to take risks)? How is your imagination affecting your confidence and motivation?

4. Purposefully use your imagined experience to enhance your performance when facing new challenges. When facing problems that provoke your imagination, choose to keep your images constructive, reasonably realistic, and positive. This will take work, because it will likely mean changing ingrained, habitual ways of thinking—here the practice of self-leadership (e.g., using the strategies presented in Chapter 3) becomes important in working to achieve yet further improvements in your self-leadership abilities.

Thought Patterns

Our life is what our thoughts make it.

—MARCUS AURELIUS

The previous discussion addressed several factors that help shape our unique psychological worlds. One way of picturing these ideas is to view our internal psychological selves in terms of thought patterns. That is, we tend to develop certain ways of thinking about our experiences. We might say that just as we develop habitual ways of behaving, we develop habitual ways of thinking. These thought patterns involve—among other things—our beliefs, our imagined experiences, and our self-talk. Figure 6-1 presents these ideas pictorially. It shows how our beliefs, our imagined experiences, and our self-talk influence one another and help shape our thought patterns. Of course, these factors are influenced by external forces such as our past experiences. The primary idea, however, is that we each construct a unique concept of life in our minds that influences our actions and how we feel about things.

Notice also in Figure 6-1 that behavior is included as an influence and a result of our thought patterns. Considerable debate and controversy have occurred recently over, essentially, a "chicken-or-egg" issue: Does our psychological makeup (e.g., attitudes, beliefs) cause our behavior, or does our behavior cause our psychological makeup? The logical answer is a bit facetious, but it is yes, they cause each other. Thus, an optimal approach to improving our self-leadership includes a focus on both. Indeed, considerable evidence suggests that if we change our behavior, we change ourselves psychologically. If we behave in a more courteous and friendly manner toward others, we are likely to change psychologically into more courteous and friendly people.

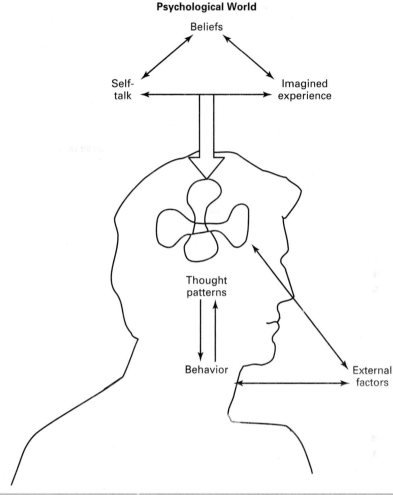

Psychological World

Beliefs

Self-talk

Imagined experience

Thought patterns

Behavior

External factors

FIGURE 6-1   Our Psychological Worlds

So let's spend a little more time thinking about how we think. Take a moment to complete the short self-assessment exercise in Table 6-1.

Interpreting Your Score

The short exercise you have just completed was designed to help you assess your current pattern of thinking. It focuses on two distinct types of thinking patterns discussed later in this chapter: opportunity thinking and obstacle thinking. The scores that you recorded for column I and column II (the maximum possible total for either is 10) suggest your current thinking tendencies. If your column I total was higher than column II, your score indicates that your current thinking patterns tend to reflect opportunity thinking more than obstacle thinking. (The reverse would be true if your column II total was higher than column I.) The greater the difference is between the two totals, the more you tend toward one pattern or the other. In general, a higher score in

TABLE 6-1   Self-Assessment Exercise: Opportunity Thinking versus Obstacle Thinking

Choose the letter of the statement (a or b) that you agree with more for each pair presented (1 through 10).

1. a. A real opportunity is built into every problem. _____
   b. Anything that can go wrong will. _____
2. a. A bird in the hand is worth two in a tree.
   b. Real opportunities are worth sticking your neck out for. _____
3. a. Most people cannot be counted on.
   b. Every person is a valuable resource in some way. _____
4. a. Difficulties make us grow.
   b. Difficulties beat us down. _____
5. a. The world is full of impossibilities.
   b. Nothing is impossible that we can conceive of. _____
6. a. When half of the days in an enjoyable vacation have passed, I still have half of my vacation to enjoy.
   b. When half of the days in an enjoyable vacation have passed, my vacation is half over. _____
7. a. The best approach to dealing with energy shortages is conservation.
   b. The best approach to dealing with energy shortages is to develop new energy sources. _____
8. a. Life after death.
   b. Death after life. _____
9. a. Failure is an opportunity to learn.
   b. Failure is a negative outcome to effort. _____
10. a. Happiness is the absence of problems.
    b. Problems are the spice of life. _____

Directions for scoring. Circle the choice you made (a or b) for each pair of statements (1 through 10). Total the number of letters circled in each column.

	I	II
1.	a	b
2.	b	a
3.	b	a
4.	a	b
5.	b	a
6.	a	b
7.	b	a
8.	a	b
9.	a	b
10.	b	a
TOTAL	_____	_____
	opportunity thinking	obstacle thinking

column I than column II reflects some desirable self-leadership tendencies, and a higher score in column II might indicate some fundamental problems.

As was the case for the self-assessment questionnaires in Chapters 3 and 4, your results on this exercise should be interpreted cautiously. The way you score might reflect your current mood or outlook as opposed to any long-term tendencies. On the other hand, an exercise such as this is useful in helping you reflect on the pattern of thought that you tend to adopt in thinking about and approaching situations.

OPPORTUNITY OR OBSTACLE THINKING: AN EXAMPLE

Two types of thought patterns that a person could adopt are what might be called opportunity thinking and obstacle thinking. Opportunity thinking involves a pattern of thoughts that focus on the opportunities and possibilities that situations or challenges hold. Creative, innovative individuals who contribute to the major breakthroughs and advances in our world most likely possess this sort of pattern of thinking. Their beliefs, their imagined future experiences, and their self-talk probably spur them on to undertake new opportunities. Obstacle thinking, on the other hand, involves a focus on the roadblocks and pitfalls of undertaking new ventures. Such a mental pattern fosters avoidance of challenges in favor of more secure actions, often with substantially lesser potential payoffs.

Skiwear mogul Klaus Obermeyer is a classic example of an opportunity thinker. Obermeyer is founder of Obermeyer Ski Apparel, a company that earned more than $30 million in 1995 despite the fact that Obermeyer went skiing every day of the ski season. He says his company originated when he saw an opportunity.[1]

> It's very simple . . . I was making $10 a day teaching skiing, but people kept canceling because of the cold. If I wanted to keep my class, I had to make them comfortable.

Obermeyer clearly viewed the fact "that his students were canceling because of the cold" as an opportunity and not an obstacle. Indeed, in 1950, he made history by tearing up his bed comforter and stitching the world's first quilted goosedown parka. He also provided the first turtleneck in the United States and the first mirrored sunglasses. As Obermeyer reasons:[2]

> People skied in knickerbockers and neckties back then. It was cold as hell. They got frostbite. They got sunburned. And their feet hurt because boots didn't fit. But all these problems were opportunities.

Another example of the benefits of opportunity thinking involves a woman named Helen Thayer. In March 1988, Ms. Thayer was on a journey that few believed could be accomplished—a solo trek to the North Magnetic Pole—a first for a woman. She had only 1 week left in her grueling exploration when an unexpected storm developed, blowing most of her remaining supplies away except seven small handfuls of walnuts and a pint of water. Thus, she would have to adjust from living off 5,000 calories a day to 100 calories. Did she make it to her destination? Yes, she certainly did! How did she manage to finish her incredible feat? Her will to win and the power of her mind were her strategic weapons against the brutal elements—the wind, the cold, the man-eating polar bears. As Ms. Thayer remarked in her book, *Polar Dream*:[3]

> I found it to be a decided advantage to accept what I had and feel grateful for it rather than wish I had more. Wishing only made me feel even more hungry and thirsty, whereas acceptance and gratitude allowed me to channel my energy into moving ahead at a good pace.

Ms. Thayer practiced opportunity thinking to help her accomplish her goal. Instead of viewing her loss of supplies as an obstacle toward her completion of her trek, she viewed the loss as an opportunity to help her focus her energy to finish the journey.

Each of us can possess both opportunity and obstacle thinking at different times and when faced with different situations. Some undertakings pose too much personal risk and should be avoided. On the other hand, we often find ourselves caught up in difficult situations unexpectedly. Because avoiding the situation is no longer a choice, the issue becomes one of how to deal with it. We probably tend to rely on certain thought patterns more than others in dealing with life's challenges. For example, should we seek worthwhile challenges because they help us grow, or should we do our best to avoid as much as possible problems of any kind? Should our thoughts be that the world is cruel and unfair, or that the world is basically good and that honest effort is rewarded? The pattern that our thinking takes influences our actions, our satisfaction with life, and our personal effectiveness.

One final example reveals that even presidents of the United States can benefit from seeing challenging situations as opportunities. On March 30, 1981, then President Ronald Reagan was wounded in the chest by a would-be assassin's bullet. The horror of the situation was a shock to millions around the world. Logically, one would think President Reagan would condemn the violent act and display a negative outlook in the wake of the atrocity. Instead, the president was said to have smiled through surgery. Numerous optimistic and humorous quotes from the president reached the public, which gradually helped relieve the mass tension. The victim seemed to be trying to support the safe onlookers rather than the seemingly more logical reverse. "Honey, I forgot to duck" (to his wife); "Please, say you're Republicans" (to the doctors); the attempted assassination "ruined one of my best suits" (to his daughter); and "send me to L.A., where I can see the air I'm breathing" (to the medical staff) were among the verbal or written remarks of the wounded president.

The results? The president's popularity rose to an apparent all-time high. Programs he had been working hard to push through Congress gained momentum. A short time after the incident, the president achieved his first major political triumph since taking office—Congress approved his budget. This triumph could be attributed largely to his admirable conduct in the wake of the assassination attempt.[4]

Change Can Be an "Opportunity"—So Bloom Where You Are Planted

J. Weisel once wrote, "Bloom where you are planted." What does this mean? The story of Jacques-Yves Cousteau illustrates the ultimate message of this quote.

At the age of 20, Cousteau's dream was to be a pilot. Consequently in 1930, Cousteau passed the highly competitive examinations to enter France's Naval Academy. He served in the navy and entered naval aviation school.

A near-fatal car crash at age 26 denied him his wings, and he was transferred to sea duty. Did Cousteau whine because he could no longer fly an airplane? Did he gripe about life being unfair? Did he complain about the new situation in which he was "planted"? No, he did not. In fact, he decided to use his new position (sea duty) to his advantage. He swam rigorously in the ocean to strengthen his arms, which were badly weakened by the accident.

This therapy had some unintended, yet beautiful consequences. As Cousteau noted in his 1953 book *The Silent World* (New York: Harper Collins), "sometimes we are lucky enough to know that our lives have been changed, to discard the old, embrace the new, and run headlong down an immutable course. It happened to me . . . when my eyes were opened to the sea."

Think about this for a moment. Cousteau's passion in life, and his claim to fame, was that of an underwater explorer. Cousteau's oceanographic expeditions set a plethora of milestones in marine research and led to his role as a spokesperson for the protection of the underwater environment. None of this—his expeditions, his television shows, his books, the number of lives that he impacted—probably would have happened if Cousteau had not "bloomed where he was planted." In other words, if Cousteau had not embraced the change in his life due to his tragic accident, the world might never have heard of him. If he had cried about not being able to fly and had refused his new assignment, we would be saying "Jacques who?"

How many times in our own lives when we are confronted with change do we say, "I wish I were back home," "I wish I were with my old friends," "I wish I were still doing my old job"? If right now you are living in the past and wishing you were back in a situation from years gone by, consider the story of Jacques Cousteau. Then ask yourself the question, "Am I trying to bloom where I am now planted?" If you answered in the negative, you could be missing out on something magical in your life. You could be missing out on discovering something about yourself that could dramatically enhance your life's direction. Cousteau's near-fatal accident led to him being "planted" somewhere else, somewhere new, somewhere unfamiliar to him. Rather than focusing on the life that he had to leave, he chose to "bloom" in his new environment—the ocean. This choice resulted in the discovery of who he was and what his life's passion would be. If he had chosen differently—chosen to complain about where he used to be and what could have been—his life probably would have been less fulfilling and his impact on the world less substantial. If you have recently been "replanted" in your life, perhaps due to a new job, a new relationship, a family crisis, or any type of change, what decision have you made or will you make? To bloom or not to bloom is indeed the question. It is hoped that Cousteau's life will show you the correct answer: Bloom where you are planted.

Regardless of whether you are in agreement with this president's political views or his subsequent actions in office, it is difficult to deny that his reaction to this life-threatening assault is little short of amazing. The would-be tragedy seemed to have been transformed into a powerful opportunity. The public feeling surrounding this distressful event and the president's inspiring behavior are reflected in a view expressed by one television commentator. In essence, he said, "I hope President Reagan feels better because of how bad we feel. I know how I feel. I wish I would have voted for him." Indeed, opportunities might be found in even the most unlikely of situations if only we let ourselves see them through the patterns of our thinking. The lives of Klaus Obermeyer, Helen Thayer, Ronald Reagan, and Thomas Edison serve as examples of this contention. To illustrate opportunity versus obstacle thinking, consider the following story about Thomas Edison.

> Edison's laboratory was virtually destroyed by a fire in December 1914, and the buildings were insured for only a fraction of the money that it would cost to rebuild them. At the age of sixty-seven, most of Edison's life's work went up in flames on that December night.
>
> The next morning, Edison looked at the ruins and said, "There is a great value in disaster. All our mistakes are burned up. Thank God we can start anew." Three weeks after the fire, Edison delivered his first phonograph.

Edison truly was an opportunity thinker in this case—he viewed the fire as a chance for a fresh start rather than as an excuse to quit. The question for you is, How do you view "fires" or problems in your life: as obstacles or as opportunities?[5]

This idea is exemplified by the following composite example based on the experiences of participants in our training seminars and university classes.

The Case of the Problem Employee That Was All in Her Mind

Alicia Smith was a department manager for ABC Corporation. She was generally good with her department employees, and her department consistently turned out solid performance. Recently, however, she had developed a poor relationship with one of her newer subordinates, Tim Williams. Unlike Alicia's other employees, Tim frequently questioned the instructions that Alicia provided for him. On a couple of occasions, he had even questioned some of Alicia's ideas during department meetings in front of the other employees. Alicia had become particularly frustrated with the situation and was convinced that Tim was intentionally trying to undermine her authority. She believed that he was going to have a disruptive influence on other employees and on the department's overall performance.

Alicia was having lunch with a friend and peer, Dave Sims, the manager of another department in the company. "I don't know whether to recommend he be terminated, transferred, or if I should take formal disciplinary action toward him or what," Alicia was saying in a frustrated tone. "I just know it's got to stop. I will not put up with it anymore," Alicia finished with emphasis.

"What exactly is he saying and doing?" Dave asked in a calm voice that didn't sound quite sympathetic enough to satisfy Alicia. "Is he being rude or behaving unethically or anything? Is he showing a lack of respect or refusing to do his work?"

"Well, no, not exactly," Alicia responded, looking at Dave a little suspiciously. "It's just that he's always arguing for another way of doing things as opposed to accepting my directions. In the end he does what I ask him to do and he works pretty hard at it, but he seems to resent my authority, or at least he's hesitant to accept it without putting up a fight first."

"Oh, this sounds familiar. I've had a few workers who have acted in a similar way over the years. I used to think they were fighting me, too. Don't take this the wrong way, but what I finally realized was that usually I was fighting them, not the other way around. I misunderstood the situation."

He paused and studied Alicia to see how she was taking his comments. After deciding she looked hesitant but interested, he continued. "You see, I learned through some reading and seminars I attended that we often make false assumptions and tell ourselves inaccurate things about difficult situations. After studying my situation, I realized that frequently the employees who seemed to challenge me were actually trying to contribute more than I was asking of them. They also were trying to contribute their own ideas and insights. And usually I found that if I let them think of their own ways of doing things, they ended up very committed to their work and grateful and supportive of me for having the opportunity to really contribute."

Dave proceeded to describe to Alicia a system he developed for challenging his own assumptions and self-statements to help him deal more constructively with difficult situations such as relating to "problem" subordinates. He also used visualization techniques to mentally rehearse and imagine constructive ways of dealing with his challenges. He explained, "Some of those difficult people who seem like major obstacles to performance actually represent tremendous opportunities if you can just help them constructively channel their energy and creativity."

Over another couple of lunches and a few short meetings, Dave helped Alicia understand and apply the important parts of his personal thought management system in a way that seemed most appealing and useful to her. Almost immediately she noticed improvements in her relationship with Tim. She began to see that Tim was in fact trying to contribute what he viewed as better ways of reaching high performance in his work. As Alicia began to allow Tim to pursue more of his own ideas, she was pleased to observe that many of his ideas paid off with significant results. Sometimes he made mistakes, but he worked hard to correct them. Most of all, Tim became a highly committed employee and one of Alicia's strongest supporters and performers.

As an additional benefit, Alicia gradually found increased satisfaction in her own job as she learned to manage her assumptions and self-statements about troubling situations constructively. She also worked on the mental images she pictured about challenging situations and worked to make sure that they were constructive. Over time, her employees developed a reputation for being some of the most creative and committed people in the company. Alicia no longer viewed challenging employees as personal threats but as positive opportunities. As a consequence, that's just what they became.

Spend some time thinking about how you think. What are your overall thinking habits? What kind of patterns do your beliefs, imagined experiences, and self-talk create in your thinking? Do these patterns enhance your psychological world and your performance? Do you tend to search for the opportunities, or do you tend to search for obstacles in challenges? What kind of thought patterns would you like to establish in your mind? How can you adapt your beliefs, imagined experiences, self-talk, and behavior to establish these patterns? The time you spend now sorting through questions such as these could make all the difference in how you spend your life. ■

Notes

1. *USA Today*, "Mogul Fashions: A Success Story," E2, 8 November 1996.
2. Ibid.
3. Helen Thayer, *Polar Dream: The Heroic Saga of the First Solo Journey by a Woman and Her Dog to the Pole* (New York: Dell Publishing Co. Inc., 1994): 231.
4. Ed Magnuson (reported by G. I. Barrett and N. MacNeil), "Reagan's Big Win," *Time* (May 18, 1981): 14–16.
5. Canfield and M. Hansen, *A Third Serving of Chicken Soup for the Soul* (Deerfield Beach, FL: Health Communications, 1996).

Team Self-Leadership[1]

or What You Get When You Mix Self-Leadership with a Team

When spiderwebs unite, they can tie up a lion.

— ETHIOPIAN PROVERB

If we were to end the book at this point, we would be shortchanging you. You might decide to return the book to your bookstore and ask for your money back. The good news is that there is more to conquer.

Up to this point, our discussion on self-leadership has focused on you as an individual. We understand, however, that much of the work you do on a daily basis is not work done by you alone. We realize that to accomplish many of your goals, you need to work with other people. A large majority of the work today in schools and businesses is done by a team of people as opposed to separate individuals.

Teams—self-directed teams, self-managing teams, and high-performance teams— are a new work-design innovation that has swept across the country and the rest of the world. This fact of business life is gaining in popularity, as estimates suggest that 40 to 50 percent of the workforce could be in some kind of team environment by the turn of the century.[2] Thus, chances are good that right now you are a member of a team either as a student in a university, as an employee in an organization, or even as part of a personal relationship (e.g., boyfriend, girlfriend, husband, or wife).

The introduction of empowered work teams into the workplace represents perhaps the most important new organization development since the industrial revolution. Teams already have demonstrated their ability to make major contributions to organizations in a variety of industries. Increased productivity; higher product and service quality; a better quality of work life for the employees; and reduced costs, turnover, and absenteeism are among the more salient payoffs.

Usually team members have an increased amount of responsibility and control. Teams perform many of the tasks that previously were the responsibility of management, such as conducting meetings, solving technical and personal problems, making a wide range of decisions on many issues including performance methods, and deciding who will complete which task. Successful teams are those that possess skills, equipment, and supplies they need to perform the work well.

The best teams tend to have capable and committed members who successfully combine their skills and knowledge for the good of the team. The challenge for teams is to accept and appreciate the unique contributions that each member can make while effectively combining individual member contributions for the good of the team. The key to team success is the creation of synergy—the condition whereby team members together accomplish significantly more than they could if they acted on their own. (A math example of synergy is $1 + 1 + 1 = 5$.) This definition fits well with the widely used acronym TEAM—Together Everyone Achieves More. Teams work best when their members have strong individual skills and strong group skills. How can a team obtain synergy? We argue that self-leadership plays an integral part in the answer to this question.

SELF-LEADERSHIP AND TEAMS

You might be thinking, "Don't the terms *self-leadership* and *teams* contradict or oppose each other?" In other words, what does leading oneself have to do with working as a team? These words are closely related. Self-leadership is just as important when you are working in a team as when you are working alone. To reach your individual potential while working within a team, you still must lead yourself. In fact, only by effectively leading yourself as a team member can you help the team lead itself, reach *its* potential, and thus achieve synergy. The act of the team leading itself describes the concept of team self-leadership.

> The application of mental and behavioral self-leadership strategies that enable team members to provide themselves with self-direction and self-motivation, and ultimately to become effective, personally empowered contributors to their team.

According to this definition, team self-leadership is similar to individual self-leadership in that they both involve the use of behavioral and mental strategies. Next we will examine some of these team-based self-leadership strategies.[3]

BEHAVIORAL ASPECTS OF TEAM SELF-LEADERSHIP

Specific behavioral team self-leadership practices include team self-observation, team self-goal-setting, team cue modification, team self-reward/self-punishment, and team rehearsal (practice).

Team Self-Observation

At the team level, self-observation represents the team's collective effort to purposefully observe (and record) its behavior and performance, as well as attempt to understand the antecedents and consequences associated with those actions. Self-observation should be done by the team. Thus, team self-observation encompasses the group working collectively to measure and understand its behavior. An example is the group seeking information needed to compare its performance with its production goals.

Team Self-Goal-Setting

Individuals can have personal goals that are coordinated with and necessary for achieving team goals, but the focus for teams is the shared goals of the team as a whole. Team goal-setting accordingly requires the group as a collective (rather than an individual leader) to establish the goals. Goal-setting by the group thus represents an element of self-leadership for the team that will encompass, but is not defined by, individual goals of team members or leaders.

Team Cue Modification

Teams can remove things that cue undesirable behavior and increase exposure to elements that cue desirable behavior. By changing environmental conditions that affect behavior, team self-leadership occurs. These attempts to change the environment are collectively performed by the team and are not synonymous with individual attempts to modify antecedents that cue behavior. An example is the team deciding to alter the configuration of its work space.

Team Self-Reward and Self-Punishment

Teams can reinforce their own behaviors by providing rewards to one another and to the group as a whole that strengthen or increase those behaviors. These rewards can be tangible or intangible. Tangible rewards can include monetary bonuses, time off, or purchasing new equipment. Intangible rewards can include increased satisfaction, joy from working as a team, or a feeling of respect for the work accomplished by the team. Punishment involves applying negative consequences to reduce undesirable behaviors. An example of punishment is a team deciding that everyone must work late to make up for excessive socialization. To be considered team self-influence, the group must administer and receive rewards and sanctions collectively. It is important to note that as with individual self-leadership, team self-punishment is neither the preferred nor the most effective method to influence a team's behavior.

Team Rehearsal

As discussed, rehearsal or practice is another step associated with the self-leadership process. Rehearsal also can be conducted either overtly or covertly by teams. An example of rehearsal might be several team members practicing a presentation they must make to the rest of the organization. This practice must be initiated and directed by the team as a whole rather than by an individual team member.

MENTAL ASPECTS OF TEAM SELF-LEADERSHIP

An underlying assumption of the discussion of mental team self-leadership strategies is the emergence of a group pattern of thinking, which is more than the existence of a simple collection of separate individual minds. This notion of a "group mind" has been further asserted by various researchers.[4] For example, W. R. Bion asserted that a group's mind-set exists beyond that of the individual group members in that the group's mind-set connects group members by an unconscious implied agreement.[5]

Accordingly, the basic premise of mental team self-leadership, similar to self-leading individuals, is that teams can enhance their performance through the collective application of specific mental strategies that result in a team mode of thinking. These collective mental strategies include beliefs and assumptions, self-talk, and mental imagery. As with our representation of individual mental self-leadership, these components of collective mental strategies interact reciprocally to influence thought patterns (but in this case, the thought patterns of the team).

Team Beliefs and Assumptions

Recall our earlier discussion of individual beliefs and assumptions. We suggested that distorted thoughts are based on some common dysfunctional beliefs and assumptions that are activated by potentially troubling situations. Most types of individual-level beliefs involved have corresponding analogs at the group level.

For example, recall the individual-level dysfunctional assumption "extreme" thinking, which referred to the tendency for individuals to evaluate things in extreme black or white categories. Similarly, a group can develop extreme beliefs. To illustrate, if a risk does not seem overwhelmingly dangerous, the team as a whole might be inclined to minimize its importance and proceed without further preparation instead of developing contingency plans in case the risk materializes.

Team Self-Talk

Earlier we described individual self-talk as what we tell ourselves, and suggested that one's self-talk can impact his or her effectiveness. In the same manner, group self-talk might significantly influence group performance. For example, within a cohesive team is a tendency for members to put social pressure on any member who expresses opinions that deviate from the group's dominant form of dialogue. This pressure is exerted by other group members to ensure that the deviant member does not disrupt the consensus of the group as a whole. This tendency toward group-enforced conformity dialogue (group self-talk) might lead to defective decision making on the part of the group (see the discussion of groupthink later in this chapter).

Team Mental Imagery

A team could potentially enhance its performance by utilizing group mental imagery to establish a common vision. Because members of successful groups tend to share a common vision, self-managing teams faced with strategic decisions should benefit from interactively creating a common image regarding what they want to accomplish, as well as visualizing effective means for doing so.

Thought Patterns

Like individuals, teams also can develop thought patterns. In other words, a team can be an opportunity or obstacle thinker. An example of team opportunity or obstacle thinking can involve the group's perception of its ability to overcome a particular challenge. If a team is faced with a technical problem that affects the quality of its product, it can view this occurrence as an opportunity to focus the group's energies and to utilize the decision-making and technical skills of the team, or as an obstacle that will prevent the team from producing a product of high quality. If the work team believes that this technical problem is an insurmountable obstacle, then it is practically assured that the product's quality will suffer. On the other hand, if the team feels that this technical problem is an opportunity to improve the product further, the probability of producing a high-quality product is enhanced. Thus, if the team believes problems are opportunities to overcome challenges, rather than obstacles that will lead to failure, the team's performance should be enhanced.

TEAM SELF-LEADERSHIP STILL MEANS INDIVIDUAL SELF-LEADERSHIP

Now that we have briefly described specific team self-leadership strategies, we recall an important point mentioned earlier in this chapter: You must effectively lead yourself as a team member if you want to help the team lead itself, reach its potential, and thus achieve synergy.

To explore this concept more fully, consider the following story.[6]

> A French scientist, Jean-Henri Fabre, had a very interesting passion in life—the study of caterpillars. At one point in his research, he conducted an experiment that involved processionary caterpillars—wormlike creatures that travel in long, unwavering lines, at the same pace and cadence. Dr. Fabre placed a group of these wormy creatures onto the thin rim of a large flowerpot, forming a circle of caterpillars, so that the leader of the group of caterpillars was nose to tail with the last caterpillar in the slow, nonending procession. Even for Dr. Fabre it was difficult to figure out who was the leader and who were the followers. For an entire day Dr. Fabre watched the caterpillars endlessly circle the rim of the flowerpot. Dr. Fabre then went home for the night, and in the morning when he arrived at his laboratory he noticed that the caterpillars were still circling the pot. Then, in the center of the flowerpot, Dr. Fabre placed a supply of food. But this did not detour the caterpillars. They never stopped circling—not even to eat. Day after day, night after night, the caterpillars paraded around and around and around and around. After seven days of parading the rim, the caterpillars finally stopped because they died of starvation and exhaustion. Not for one moment did a single caterpillar stop to look up, eat, or interrupt the circle of travel. Instead, they put their heads down and blindly followed the caterpillar ahead of them (instead of thinking maybe their way was better) until they died.

This story might parallel the challenge you have faced or will face as a member of a team. The challenge involves not acting as the caterpillars and blindly following the members of your team. By doing this, you are not practicing effective team self-leadership. To practice effective team self-leadership, you must concurrently maintain your own unique belief system and viewpoint and work together as a team. If you give up your own uniqueness and way of looking at the world by not telling the group your position on topics, then your group could end up like the helpless caterpillars. In other words, if all the members of your group blindly follow each other, then they will continue to circle, never progressing and thus never performing well. This idea does not mean that you should not try to cooperate with team members, but rather that you should work together in an effective manner. When a team works together, it is productive to disagree and constructively discuss different views. Only by discussing aloud differing views can your team develop the ideal way to approach a task or problem. Only by maintaining your individual viewpoint can you add to the team self-leadership of your group.

By now, you might have recognized that team self-leadership involves balance between a focus on yourself and a focus on the team. We refer to this as a balance between the "me" and the "we." By successfully maintaining this balance, you will prosper within your group and help yourself and your team members avoid acting like caterpillars.

Networking: Another Type of Self-Leading Teamwork

—Stuart Mease and David Moore

True masters of self-leadership realize that they can't achieve all of their goals on their own. They know that building a team through networking with key people can be an important self-leadership strategy.

Most would likely agree that Bill Gates is a master self-leader. He has demonstrated skill at a number of self-leadership techniques (e.g., self-goal-setting, positive self-talk, and so on). However, much of Gates's success can be credited to his personal network and perhaps even more to the network of his mother, Mary Maxwell Gates.

Mary served on the national board of the United Way with IBM's chief executive officer John Opel. When a senior manager at IBM expressed concern that Big Blue was taking a risk by entrusting the development of the DOS operating system to the then-fledging Microsoft, Opel responded, "That wouldn't be Mary's boy, Bill, would it?" Needless to say, Microsoft kept the job and one of the greatest fortunes was created. Additionally, Mary served on the boards of Unigard Security Insurance Group, US West, KIRO Incorporated, and the University of Washington.

She is not the only one in the family with a strong network. Bill's father was a prominent corporate lawyer in Seattle, as well as a former president of the Washington State Bar Association. Clearly, Bill Gates came from a family that had the kind of connections that can foster success. Although he demonstrated abilities as a computer software business genius, much of his success is the result of his ability to utilize a network of valuable connections, which is essential to becoming a master self-leader.

Networking can be defined as "connecting people to create mutually beneficial relationships." It's a skill used by individuals to bring two or more people together. The benefits of networking are infinite. Individuals who build large and diverse networks of people are able to achieve goals in a fraction of the time that it would take if they tried to achieve them on their own. They also are introduced to new opportunities that would not have existed without the networking process. For example, a common saying about succeeding in a job search is "it's not what you know, it's who you know." In support, in his book *Dig Your Well Before You Are Thirsty,* Harvey McKay states that about 70 percent of all jobs are obtained through the process of networking, and only 20 percent of all jobs are advertised.

Sincerity is essential for reaping the full benefit of networking. For example, if a leader uses networking strictly for self-serving reasons, the relationship is not likely to succeed. The leader needs to have a personal concern for each individual in the network. In other words, to truly succeed in networking a team mentality is needed, including a sincere desire to help oneself as well as others.

BALANCING THE "ME" WITH THE "WE"

A well-known proverb states: "The best potential in 'me' is 'we.'" The underlying message in this proverb is a critical aspect of team self-leadership: For you to reach your ultimate potential at school and work, you must work *with* your team and not *against* it. If team members are focused on only themselves and the credit they receive rather than focusing on the success of the team as a whole, the team members' performance and the team's overall performance will suffer.

The following story should illustrate this critical point necessary for the successful implementation of team self-leadership.[7]

> Two geese were about to start southward on their annual migration, when they were entreated by a frog to take him with them. The geese expressed their willingness to do so if a means of conveyance could be devised.
>
> The frog produced a long stalk of pond grass, got the geese each to grab an end with their beaks, while he clung to it by his mouth in the middle. In this way the three began their journey. Some farmers below noticed the strange sight. The men loudly expressed their admiration for the travel device and wondered who had been clever enough to discover it. Whereupon the vainglorious frog opened his mouth to say, "It was I," lost his grip, fell to the earth, and was dashed to pieces.

One moral to this story could be, "When you have a good thing going, keep your mouth shut" (grin). Although truth and humor can be found in this interpretation, a more applicable moral to an understanding of team self-leadership is as follows.

> Effective team self-leadership will not occur when team members place too much emphasis on themselves and worry too much about who is going to get the credit. This ideal will bring poor performance to the team members and to the team as a whole.

Conversely, team members who are committed to team self-leadership, who recognize that the best potential in "me" is "we," and who recognize that team success requires a total group effort whereby team members strive unselfishly to complete their task or project, eventually will achieve their individual goals and those of the team.

The "Me/We" Balance: Time to Start Sharing

—Craig L. Pearce
The Peter F. Drucker Graduate School of Management
Claremont Graduate University

More and more in our interconnected world, we find ourselves interacting in groups and teams. In our families, we tackle home-improvement projects; in the community, we join volunteer groups to better our environment; at work, we participate in cross-functional teams to improve the organization. The leadership challenges in our many groups and teams stretch beyond self-leadership: Once in a team, one must lead oneself as well as coordinate with, collaborate with, and rely upon others. As a result, a collection of capable self-leaders does not necessarily ensure team success.

How might one increase the chances of team success? Fully understanding leadership in the team environment is the first place to start. Recent evidence suggests that we need to move beyond the traditional models of top-down leadership to consider how leadership might be shared in teams. We label this phenomenon shared leadership. Shared leadership represents a next-generation model of leadership that holds considerable promise for helping us as we work, play, and live in teams.

What is shared leadership? Shared leadership is a dynamic interactive influence process in which team members lead one another to accomplish team goals successfully. With shared leadership, leadership comes from, and is received by, all team members such that all members of the team actively engage in the leadership of the team. This description of shared leadership lies in stark contrast with the traditional top-down leadership in which an appointed leader leads and team members simply follow.

Are you used to a strict top-down leadership style? If so, shared leadership probably sounds like some new age fad likely to induce sheer chaos. Realistically, shared leadership can wreak havoc if not properly managed. However, investigations on shared leadership in a wide variety of complex situations, such as change management, virtual, research and development, military, and top corporate executive teams, illustrate the positive and powerful impact of shared leadership. As tasks become more complex, the potential benefits of shared leadership become greater. Effective teams dealing with complex tasks must draw upon the variety of expertise available from all team members rather than simply relying on one individual to be the expert on each and every aspect. Thus, at various points in time and in various situations, the person to whom a team looks for leadership will, and should, change.

If leadership is to be shared by the team, what is the point of self-leadership? Shared leadership and self-leadership are inextricably linked because team members incapable of self-leadership also are incapable of shared leadership. For instance, effective shared leadership requires all team members to trust that each will follow through with his or her specific responsibilities; in other words, all team members need to be capable self-leaders. Equally important is the fact that capable self-leaders have the self-confidence and self-awareness to know their abilities as well as their limitations. Such clear self-knowledge enables capable self-leaders to (1) lead others when they possess the relevant knowledge; and (2) be led by others when it is others who possess the relevant expertise.

In our new, team-based environment, having a group of people who are capable self-leaders is necessary, but not sufficient, to guarantee the success of a team. The next generation of leadership requires engaging fully in shared leadership such that all team members are capable self-leaders, capable of leading others, and capable of being led.

If you are interested in learning more about shared leadership, we recommend reading *Shared Leadership: Reframing the How's and Why's of Leadership,* by Craig L. Pearce and Jay A. Conger (eds.). (Thousand Oaks, CA: Sage Publications, 2003). It contains an excellent chapter on the link between self- and shared leadership by Jeffrey Houghton, Christopher P. Neck, and Charles C. Manz, as well as several other provocative chapters on shared leadership.

To reiterate, too much "we-ness" can lead to a situation in which members act like caterpillars and blindly follow the team as a whole. Accordingly, the team is trapped in the vicious circle, neither progressing nor performing well. This type of situation, known as groupthink, is a common pitfall to team success. Groupthink refers to the tendency for groups to become overly conforming and ineffective in their decision making.[8]

Consider an example of too much "we-ness" (groupthink) in a team. Have you ever been in a team situation in which members were discussing a particular problem, and in the course of that discussion you had an important thought that went against the predominant view of most of the team? Did you remain silent or speak up? If you remained silent, you were helping your team experience groupthink—or too much "we-ness." You were not maintaining your individuality; you were not expressing your personal viewpoints. The outcome of your actions, especially if other members also were surpressing their divergent views, would likely be defective decision making and consequently poor team performance.

An effective team member in scenarios such as this one would not have remained silent. Teams that practice team self-leadership exhibit "teamthink" behaviors as opposed to groupthink behaviors. Teamthink is a situation in which team members strike a balance between themselves (the "me") and the team (the "we").[9] This teamthink balance involves members working together as a cohesive unit, but at the same time constructively disagreeing when it is necessary to do so. This type of scenario can create the earlier-mentioned concept of synergy, when the total results are greater than the sum of what each member could accomplish individually. Additionally, members in teamthink teams encourage each member to express *all* of their views and ideas so that the optimal

TABLE 7-1 Groupthink versus Teamthink

Groupthink	Teamthink
• Direct social pressure against divergent views	• Encouragement of divergent views
• Self-censorship of concerns	• Open expression of concerns/ideas
• Illusion of invulnerability to failure	• Awareness of limitations/threats
• Illusion of unanimity	• Recognition of members' uniqueness
• Self-appointed mind guards that screen out external information	• Recognition of views outside the group
• Collective efforts to rationalize	• Discussion of collective doubts
• Stereotyped views of enemy leaders	• Utilization of non-stereotypical views
• Illusion of morality	• Recognition of ethical and moral consequences of decisions

manner of performing a task or handling a problem can be determined. In short, the most effective self-leadership teams are those that demonstrate teamthink behaviors.

Table 7-1 lists the corresponding characteristics, or symptoms, of a team experiencing either teamthink or groupthink. Perhaps a real-life application could fully capture our discussion on team self-leadership. Research has highlighted organizational cases in which effective team self-leadership did or did not occur within a team setting. The following example was developed from a composite of several actual team cases.[10] Would you say that this team is practicing effective team self-leadership? Why or why not? This team seems to be engaging in groupthink behaviors and thus not demonstrating optimal team self-leadership. Several groupthink symptoms are readily displayed, especially direct pressure, self-censorship, and an illusion of unanimity. Verbal and nonverbal pressure toward conformity was applied to individuals who suggested changes, which contributed to the tendency for members to censor themselves even though they apparently disagreed with the leader's plan. Ultimately, members' behaviors created an illusion of unanimous agreement, and thus the team leader ended the meeting before any real constructive critical analysis and discussion had occurred. This concurrence-seeking process resulting from the collective thinking of the group is likely serving as a catalyst for poor team decisions and negative group outcomes. In short, the team is not an example of team self-leadership.

The members of the team looked discouraged as they stared at the graphs at the front of the room. They had just been briefed by their team leader concerning the team's performance over the previous year in producing a diagnostic ultrasound device. Their product quality had suffered recently, as evidenced by the fact that their product's mean time between failure (MTBF) had fallen far below the industry average in the highly competitive field of medical electronics. The team leader had let them know in no uncertain terms how disappointed he was with the team's performance and the way the members had been handling the situation. He went on to describe in some detail a plan he had developed for getting the team's product quality back on track.

The members of the group were well trained and for the most part experienced workers. A variety of well-informed alternative ideas for meeting the division's current challenges were contained in the minds of these competent people. Nevertheless, the discussion was surprisingly narrow. After the team leader completed his comments, team members made a couple of suggestions for minor modifications to their leader's ideas. These suggestions were met, however, with mildly disapproving stares or comments from other members, indicating that such modifications were not necessary. Most of the other reactions from the group echoed agreement and endorsement of the team leader's ideas. The minds of the engineers in this group were working as one because in reality only one mind was doing the real thinking. Several members appeared to disagree with the team leader's ideas. Most of them never spoke up. They groaned and shifted uncomfortably in their chairs, but they did not say a word. Finally, the team leader interrupted the limited discussion. Are there any other concerns about our course of action? When no one said anything, the leader commented, "I guess we're all in agreement then," and the meeting ended.

Consider the following continuation of the previous composite team case 1 year later after the team of engineers underwent several sessions of team self-leadership training.[11]

Once again, the engineers had just been briefed by their team leader concerning the team's performance over the previous year. Their product's mean time between failure (MTBF) was still down, and the team leader once again expressed disappointment concerning the team's poor performance and stated that he held each of them personally responsible. However, unlike the previous year, team members began to discuss openly and critically the situation after the manager's briefing. First, one of the engineers raised specific concerns about the team leader's proposed solution for turning things around. Then, while listening attentively and supporting each other as valued team members, several individuals constructively challenged the views of the team leader and other members. This open exchange generated a variety of alternative solutions that combined pieces of several suggestions. An atmosphere of constructive challenge developed. During the course of the meeting, each team member, at least once, discussed his or her ideas about how to increase the group's performance. In the end, the team selected a solution that was very different from the one the team leader had originally proposed, but one that the group had worked out together. Even the team leader was pleased, recognizing the superiority of the new solution. Because the engineers had naturally engaged in a teamthink process (due to their training), they now believed that they could make their adopted solution work. They focused on the challenges of implementation, encouraging one another and collectively imaging the team's ultimate successful performance.

(continued)

Many teamthink symptoms are readily displayed in this second example, especially encouragement of divergent views and open expression of ideas. This effective synergistic team thinking, if maintained, is likely to serve as a catalyst for effective decision making and enhanced team performance well into the future. Indeed, this team 1 year later is an excellent example of a team practicing effective team self-leadership.

In summary, we have attempted to show in this chapter that self-leadership and teams are not conflicting concepts. Self-leadership is not only an integral dimension of individual performance but also a key element of team success.

Self-Leadership in Work Teams

—Greg L. Stewart

Does self-leadership have a place in work teams? Many people quickly respond affirmatively to this question. However, the role of self-leadership in teams is a complex issue. Self-leadership can occur at two levels. The first level is the team, which is concerned with the extent that the team as a collective group exercises self-leadership. The second level is the individual. This level is concerned with the extent that individual team members exercise self-leadership.

Self-leadership at the team level occurs when teams engage in leadership activities that traditionally have been carried out by a manager or supervisor. Self-leading teams take responsibility for production and do things such as planning inventory schedules, ordering materials, and fixing machinery. Team members also become involved in human resources tasks such as hiring and firing team members, appraising the performance of teammates, and disciplining team members who are tardy or absent. Teams exercising advanced forms of self-leadership also take on increased work related to strategic planning, interfacing with customers, and developing new technology. Although managers frequently express concern that team members will not be effective at these tasks, research suggests that team members can indeed work together and effectively fill these roles.[12] Research also has demonstrated that team-level self-leadership is most beneficial when teams engage in creative tasks that are nonroutine.[13]

Self-leadership for individual team members takes place when they pursue self-set goals through physical and mental strategies. However, a common problem in work teams is that self-leadership for the individual can conflict with the self-leadership of the team as a whole.[14] For instance, an individual working on an automobile design team might have a goal to develop a car that has exceptional fuel efficiency. Yet, the goal of the team as a whole might be to develop a high-performance car that is not necessarily efficient. Individual team members also might want to exercise self-leadership by spending evenings with family and friends rather than working. What if this is in opposition to the team's collective goal of increasing their productivity? In the end, effective self-leading teams need to find a balance between team and individual self-leadership. Individual team members must be allowed the freedom and responsibility to pursue their personal goals, but those goals at some level need to align with the collective goals of the team.

One effective method of balancing team and individual self-leadership appears to be training team members in the area of conflict management. There are two types of conflict. Relational conflict occurs when people have interpersonal disagreements. Task conflict occurs when team members have disagreements about the tasks that they are doing. Relationship conflict is seldom helpful, but moderate amounts of task conflict are beneficial.[15] Effective self-leading teams are thus trained to avoid relationship conflict but to allow individual team members to exercise self-leadership and openly express their viewpoints, ideas, and opinions. Team members also must develop trust in one another so that task conflict does not become relationship conflict.[16] An effective balance of team and individual self-leadership is, therefore, most likely to occur when team norms (informal guidelines for appropriate behavior) encourage moderate amounts of task conflict but discourage personal attacks that destroy trust and relationships.

Notes

1. Many of the ideas in this chapter have been adapted from material in C. Manz, C. Neck, J. Mancuso, and K. Manz, *For Team Members Only: Making Your Workplace Team Productive and Hassle-Free* (New York: Amacom, 1997).

2. Manz et al., 1997.

3. Our discussion of the behavioral and mental aspects of team self-leadership has been adapted from C. P. Neck, G. Stewart, and C. Manz, "Self-Leaders Within Self-Leading Teams: Toward an Optimal Equilibrium" in M. Beyerlein, D. Johnson, and S. Beyerlein (eds.), *Advances in Interdisciplinary Studies of Work Teams* 3 (Greenwich, CT: JAI Press, 1996): 43–65.

4. For an extended discussion of the group mind concept, please see C. P. Neck and C. C. Manz, "From Groupthink to Teamthink: Toward the Creation of Constructive Thought Patterns in Self-Managing Work Teams," *Human Relations* 47 (1994): 929–952.

5. See W. R. Bion, Experience in Groups (New York: Basic Books, 1961).

6. Adapted from G. VanEkeren, *The Speaker's Sourcebook* (Upper Saddle River, NJ: Prentice Hall, 1988).

7. B. Cavanaugh, *More Sower's Seeds* (Mahwah, NJ: Paulist Press, 1992).

8. For a detailed discussion of groupthink, see I. L. Janis, *Groupthink* (Boston: Houghton Mifflin, 1983).

9. For an extended discussion of the teamthink and groupthink concepts, see C. P. Neck and C. C. Manz, "From Groupthink to Teamthink: Toward the Creation of Constructive Thought Patterns in Self-Managing Work Teams," *Human Relations* 47 (1994): 929–952; and C. C. Manz and C. P. Neck, "Teamthink: Beyond the Groupthink Syndrome in Self-Managing Work Teams," *Journal of Managerial Psychology* 10 (1995): 7–15.

10. This case was adapted from material in C. C. Manz and C. P. Neck, "Teamthink: Beyond the Groupthink Syndrome in Self-Managing Work Teams," *Journal of Managerial Psychology* 10 (1995): 7–15.

11. This continuation of the case was adapted from material in C. C. Manz and C. P. Neck,

"Teamthink: Beyond the Groupthink Syndrome in Self-Managing Work Teams," *Journal of Managerial Psychology* 10 (1995): 7–15.

12. C. C. Manz, and H. P. Sims, Jr. (1987). "Leading Workers to Lead Themselves: The External Leadership of Self-Managing Work Teams." *Administrative Science Quarterly* 32: 106–128.

13. G. L. Stewart and M. R. Barrick (2000). "Team Structure and Performance: Assessing the Mediating Role of Intrateam Process and the Moderating Role of Task Type." *Academy of Management Journal* 43: 135–148.

14. J. R. Barker (1993). "Tightening the Iron Cage: Concertive Control in Self-Managing Teams." *Administrative Science Quarterly* 38: 408–437.

15. K. A. Jehn (1997). "A Qualitative Analysis of Conflict Types and Dimensions in Organizational Groups." *Administrative Science Quarterly* 42: 530–557.

16. T. L. Simons and R. S. Peterson (2000). "Task Conflict and Relationship Conflict in Top Management Teams: The Pivotal Role of Intragroup Trust." *Journal of Applied Psychology* 85: 102–111.

Reviewing Travel Tales of Previous Journeys

or Examples of Self-Leadership in Practice

> *Let everyone sweep in front of [their] own door
> and the whole world will be clean.*
>
> —GOETHE

Many examples of applications of the self-leadership ideas brought together in this book are available. An attempt will be made here to present some of these examples. Thousands of participants in our training workshops and college courses have applied strategies presented in this book to their own problems and challenges according to their own self-designed plans. These experiences formed the basis for many of the examples shared throughout. The purpose of this chapter is to provide further real-life support for the argument that self-leadership techniques and strategies offer many potential benefits when effectively and systematically practiced. The discussion will touch briefly on three categories of self-leadership application: (1) personal problems, (2) athletics, and (3) organizational/work problems. Applications to personal problems and athletics will be discussed briefly before addressing the primary focus of this book: organizational/work/school challenges. It is hoped that the combination of these different types of applications will provide a better picture of the wide applicability and potential of self-leadership strategies.

SELF-LEADERSHIP APPLIED TO PERSONAL PROBLEMS

Probably the most extensive application of systematic, self-regulatory strategies has occurred in the field of psychology.[1] More specifically, major strides have been made in developing the ability of individuals to deal more effectively with their own problems. Specific difficulties that have been addressed are too numerous to discuss fully here. Instead, a brief comment will be made on a sampling of self-leadership applications to personal problems. It is useful to look at these examples first because much of the idea development that is included in this book ultimately can be traced to psychology-based applications to personal problems.

Consider the challenge of controlling eating behavior when confronted with a weight problem. Various strategies have been applied, many with impressive success, to deal with this difficulty. One original approach, for example, involved various cueing strategies. The logic employed was that many dysfunctional eating behaviors stem from personal exposure to dysfunctional cues in our environment. Because cues such as watching television, reading, and socializing often become associated with eating, one way of controlling eating is to control these cues. Thus, numerous individuals have benefited (lost substantial weight) by restricting their eating to only a limited number of infrequent situations (e.g., dinnertime) and purposefully not eating in other situations that potentially could become a cue to future eating (watching television.)

Similar techniques also have been applied to smoking behavior, with significant success (in reducing smoking) in many cases. One particularly interesting example employed the use of a specially designated smoking chair that was located in unpleasant surroundings (e.g., the garage). By limiting smoking only to this chair, many other potential cues (e.g., watching television, drinking a cup of coffee at the dinner table) for smoking behavior are eliminated.

Many other self-regulatory strategies have been applied to these dysfunctional, habitual behaviors. By altering self-statements regarding weight loss (e.g., "I've been torturing myself with starvation and I'm just not losing much weight" to "I'm making progress. I'm losing pounds slowly but surely"), many individuals have reported beneficial results. Similarly, self-reinforcement for improving eating habits has been of significant help to those who are trying to lose weight. A nice dinner out (nutritionally balanced, of course) as a reward for achieving a weight loss goal (e.g., losing 10 pounds) can provide incentive for future weight loss. Various forms of imagery (e.g., imagining negative results such as excessive weight problems or cancer) also have been used in the treatment of eating and smoking problems.

One particularly interesting application of imagined experience has been made to a type of interpersonal behavior—assertiveness.[2] Specifically, individuals were instructed to imagine scenes that called for them to be assertive and to imagine positive results from their assertive behavior. Individuals might imagine themselves in a restaurant, for example, receiving a steak cooked medium well when they ordered it medium rare. They would then imagine themselves sending the steak back and asking to receive another one cooked as they ordered it (medium rare). Finally, they would imagine receiving an excellent steak just as they wanted, and receiving other positive results (such as the manager making a reduction to the total amount on their check because of their inconvenience) stemming from their assertiveness. Systematic use of imagery, such as that described, over a period of time was found to benefit many individuals by helping them increase significantly their subsequent assertiveness.

APPLICATIONS IN ATHLETICS

Many self-leadership techniques also have been applied, in various forms, to athletics.[3] Reflecting this emphasis, several articles (combined into a special feature focusing on the psychological and social aspects of physical activity) were published in the *Journal of Physical Education, Recreation and Dance* (March 1982). Interestingly, the material presented in these articles closely parallels several of the major themes of this book.

(The material emphasizes strategies such as self-observation, self-goal-setting, and rehearsal; it focuses directly on important behaviors; it addresses the importance of natural enjoyment of activities derived from feelings of competence and personal control; and it argues for the importance of thought patterns established through effective use of imagery, self-talk, and essentially positive, or opportunity, thinking.)

A comprehensive review of the extensive applications of self-leadership strategies to athletic activity is beyond the scope of this book. Indeed, a growing area known as *sport psychology* has provided much knowledge on the subject. It is instructive, however, to review some particularly interesting examples for illustrative purposes. The use of self-set goals is one strategy that is especially relevant to athletics. Whether the goal involves field-goal percentage for a basketball player, completing the mile in a specific time for a runner, or achieving a specified score for 18 holes of golf, self-goal-setting can provide athletes with direction for their efforts. Some athletes set goals that are too high, however, so they cannot possibly achieve them. It is important that goals be challenging, but achievable.

For athletes, this frequently means that the focus needs to be on process-related goals such as effort, form, and strategy rather than on the outcome of a contest. In young soccer players, for example, evidence shows that stress, which can undermine the natural enjoyment of a recreational activity, results from individual perceptions of an inability to meet performance demands.[4] Because competition usually means that someone or some team has to lose (and usually that means 50 percent of those participating), goals focusing on winning might not be particularly effective. In many cases, athletes might do their best but simply do not possess the ability to beat outstanding opponents.

An especially intriguing area of self-leadership application to athletics focuses on the creative use of imagery to facilitate desirable performance. A review of 60 different sports studies across a wide range of activities and ages of performers found a consistent positive relationship between constructive mental imagery and performance.[5] For example, one author commented on a highly successful golf instructor and a well-known professional golfer who both strongly advocated that players should picture the ideal golf swing in their mind to improve their game.[6] The logic employed is that if players can imagine themselves smoothly and cleanly performing a golf shot that accomplishes what they desire (and they do this before swinging), the result is likely to be a more natural and effective shot.

A similar process has been used in many other sports, as well. According to reports, certain Olympic gymnasts, for example, employ imagery as an aid to performance.[7] One gymnast said that before an event, she imagines what she sees when she performs. Another explained that she feels the motion in her muscles as though performing. Likewise, at least one world-class high jumper has employed imagery: If he could mentally picture himself slowly floating over the bar, he knew he could make the jump. A highly successful swimming team at a major state university employs imagined experience as part of its preparation for competition. Swimmers are encouraged to imagine the race, including the feeling of the water on their bodies, their strokes, breathing, and so forth before the race begins.

Also, the overall pattern of thinking that an athlete brings to a sport appears to be especially important. Terms that are frequently used in reference to competitions, such as getting "psyched up" or being "psyched out," reflect the importance many place on this critical role. Recall our earlier story about Olympic gold medalist Dan O'Brien. His change in thinking was a catalyst toward his winning the Olympic decathalon. The need for athletes to believe in their ability to perform and to engage in facilitative rather than destructive thoughts might be in many cases as important as physical practice and preparation. The idea of "psychological barriers" to performance in athletics is an interesting example.[8] The 4-minute mile, the 7-foot high jump, and the 18-foot pole vault are examples of the obstacles to athletic achievement that are as much psychologically as physically based. Interestingly, some evidence suggests that if weight lifters are deceived into believing that they are lifting less weight than they actually are, they are able to lift significantly more weight than they could otherwise.[9] Recall from Chapter 5 our discussion about the Russian Olympian, Vasily Alexeev. He is indeed an example of this psychological phenomenon in the world of weight lifting. The need for athletes to focus on the positive aspects of an event and to engage in constructive rather than destructive self-statements (e.g., "I've practiced hard and I can do well" rather than "I hope I don't blow it; I'm just not sure I can do it") has been emphasized.[10] Remember that, according to Roger Banister (the first man to run the mile in less than 4 minutes), a major reason why so many have now run a less-than-4-minute mile is because runners finally came to *believe* that it could be done.

APPLICATIONS IN WORK/ORGANIZATIONAL SITUATIONS

Systematic attempts to apply self-leadership methods to work organizations are still at a relatively early stage of development. Nonetheless, examples of innovative applications are available that indicate a great deal of promise. These examples can be found across a wide range of organizational positions, including uniquely autonomous jobs that are particularly suited for and in need of self-leadership (e.g., salespersons, dentists, medical doctors, auditors, college professors, and elementary and high school teachers), managers in organizations, and nonmanagement workers. Some of these applications will be discussed briefly to reflect the progress that has been made, as well as the vast potential for the future.

UNIQUELY AUTONOMOUS JOBS

Uniquely autonomous jobs in organizations are of special interest for self-leadership study. Certainly salespersons who spend a great deal of time traveling by themselves and calling on customers find that to a large degree they must be their own managers. Training in sales techniques and an expression of confidence in their abilities by the home office are often not enough for many to handle this challenge successfully. In the short run, for example, treating themselves to an expensive dinner for closing a big sale might be the only material reward they receive until returning home from a trip in the field. Salespersons need to play a critical role in their own development, motivation, and systematic self-leadership. Setting personal goals, rehearsing sales presentations, administering self-rewards, and seeking the natural rewards in their job could mean the difference between success and failure.

Indeed, many other jobs present similar challenges—from the loosely supervised machine operator on a midnight shift to the chief executive officer of a large corporation who has ultimate authority for the direction of a business. Our own lines of work, a college professor and a consultant, demand a high level of self-leadership. Yet our experience has revealed numerous cases in our profession in which individuals (including ourselves) have had personal and professional setbacks because of ineffective self-leadership practices. These setbacks often result from setting unrealistic goals, being overly self-critical, and engaging in dysfunctional thought patterns (e.g., inaccurate, debilitating, imagined experiences relating to immediate behavior choices).

To explore more fully the role of self-leadership for individuals who are in highly autonomous positions, one especially challenging type of job will be singled out as an example—the entrepreneur. For our purposes, an entrepreneur can be described as an owner-manager of a firm who sets its course and largely determines its fate: success or failure. Entrepreneurs are in a difficult position, because they must, largely on their own, beat the staggering odds against new business ventures. (It has been estimated that as few as 1 out of 100 survive 3 years.) Research does in fact suggest that entrepreneurs who effectively utilize the mental self-leadership strategies previously discussed (e.g., self-talk, mental imagery) will be more successful than those who do not.[11] Also, Dr. Charles Snyder and Charles Manz have conducted a series of personal interviews with several successful entrepreneurs (i.e., those who have survived, against all odds, longer than 3 years and were currently doing well) operating a wide range of businesses.[12] They found that although these entrepreneurs might downplay the use of any systematic management strategies on their part, they displayed several common threads of a systematic self-leadership fabric in their behavior. A few of the self-leadership applications they revealed follow.

Consider Mr. Air (the name is changed to protect confidentiality), the majority stock owner and manager of a commuter airline in the southern United States. Mr. Air uses the strategy of self-observation, for example, by keeping a daily log (a detailed record of how he spends his time). He also keeps a record of what he says to others over the phone regarding business matters to help him be consistent in his future dealings with these people. Mr. Air has adopted various cueing strategies to help manage himself. He uses a chalkboard directly in front of his desk, for example, to record notes that serve as a reminder and a guide for his work efforts. He also makes use of self-applied and natural rewards. He enjoys reviewing his performance and feeling good about (he mentally rewards himself for) his achievements and, in general, just seems to get a kick out of (experiences the natural rewards of) what he is doing. (He even continues to exercise his pilot's prerogative by taking a turn at flying some of the airline's routes.)

Perhaps the most striking feature of Mr. Air's approach to his work is his eye for opportunities. Many of his competitors have gone out of business, yet he is determined to expand to take advantage of new opportunities rather than reduce services. In fact, shortly before our interview, Mr. Air had worked out a creative financial plan, despite low funds, to buy a larger airplane. He was exuberant, and rightly so, as he told us of this accomplishment. He didn't need us to tell him that this was quite an achievement—it was apparent from the satisfied expression on his face and the energetic tone of his voice that he had already taken care of that himself. As he put it, "Self-gratification—that's what it's all about."

Mr. Air is just one of many successful entrepreneurs who, although seeming to be unaware that they are doing so, reveal obvious signs of systematic self-leadership practice. Consider Mr. Notes, the owner-manager of a successful company in the Midwest that distributes synopses of college textbooks. He relies heavily on self-set goals to help him direct his own behavior and facilitate the success of his business. Particularly in the early days of his business, he found goals to be invaluable in directing his efforts toward the development of his company and to serve as a basis for exercising another self-leadership strategy—self-reward. More specifically, Mr. Notes has found providing monetary bonuses for himself contingent on achieving sales goals to be an effective strategy for facilitating his performance.

Mr. Restaurant (the owner of a small family restaurant), on the other hand, found posting checklists (a cueing strategy) to be a useful method of ensuring that he, as well as other employees, consistently follow established procedures and maintain acceptable levels of performance. In addition, when important performance goals are achieved, Mr. Restaurant and his employees close up and throw a party for themselves.

Mr. Sport, the owner-manager of a sporting goods store, combines the strategies of self-goal-setting and self-observation to manage himself. He sets 2-year goals and records them on a checklist (a self-observation strategy), enabling him to make additions and deletions and keep track of delays in goal attainment. He is always searching for new goals and frequently breaks longer-term goals into more immediate targets for his daily efforts. Mr. Sport also reported an especially powerful self-reward process that helps him maintain his motivation. As he accomplishes goals and reviews his own performance favorably, he feels a "rush of adrenaline" and experiences a "terrific high." Indeed, Mr. Sport appears to be urged onward by a combination of internal self-praise and the natural rewards of succeeding on the job.

ORGANIZATIONAL MANAGEMENT POSITIONS

Managers are well suited for systematic self-leadership practice. Organizational research, as well as personal experience and observation, has made us acutely aware of the difficult challenges that require managers to be especially good self-managers. If not, then managers can easily become poor managers of others and of organizational resources. For many, the fast-paced, multifaceted demands of a management position can become overwhelming. As phones ring off the hook, subordinates wait for their attention, multiple deadlines stare them in the face, a seemingly endless onslaught of meetings compete for their time, and they are snowed under by a mountain of information and "urgent" demands, the manager's potential for ineffectiveness and inefficiency is enormous. Peter Drucker has described effectiveness as "doing the right thing" and efficiency as "doing things right."[13] In essence, a manager—despite typically being in a sizable organization that imposes guidelines and constraints, and offers various incentives—must largely choose among his vast demands, what to spend time on, and how to expend effort on the tasks chosen. Self-leadership practices of managers can be instrumental in determining whether they are doing the right things and doing them correctly.

Mental Self-Leadership Training: Teaching Employees to Lead Themselves
An example of how self-leadership can be taught occurred at America West
Airlines. America West, an international commercial airline, employs approximately 12,100 people and is based in Phoenix, Arizona. We recently attempted to
teach various employees of America West to utilize mental self-leadership strategies to enhance their work lives. An interesting aspect of the training situation was
that just prior to beginning the training, the airline had declared bankruptcy. As a
result of this critical financial situation, America West management laid off 2,000
workers and reduced its fleet of aircraft from 115 to 100 planes. Consequently,
many of the employees of America West were fearful of losing their jobs.

Exactly what does self-leadership of thought training involve? Let's take a
closer look at this training program. Trainees received instruction on the utilization of the following mental strategies to enhance their performance: (1) self-talk,
(2) mental imagery, (3) managing beliefs and assumptions, (4) thought patterns,
and (5) relapse prevention. The training program consisted of six 2-hour sessions.
Within each session, the focus included the following: (1) definition of the mental
self-leadership strategies, (2) examples of real-life applications, (3) specific/rele-
vant on-the-job applications, and (4) relapse prevention (to ensure maintenance
of the learned skills). Multiple training media designed to reinforce the learning of
the mental self-leadership strategies were utilized including instructor lectures,
video presentations, and individual and group exercises.

The first session served as an introduction to establish rapport and create
interest with the trainees and to provide a general overview of the principles of
thought self-leadership. The second session was directed toward describing the
link between an individual's distorted thoughts and his or her beliefs and
assumptions. Trainees were taught to identify their cognitive distortions and to
replace these distortions with more functional forms of thought.

The third session focused on self-dialogue. The primary thrust of this session was replacing negative self-talk with that of a more constructive and positive
nature. The fourth session involved the concept of mental imagery. In this session,
trainees were taught to follow specific mental imagery steps to complete assignments on the job and outside of work more effectively.

In the fifth session, the training focused on the concept of thought patterns.
The basis of the thought pattern training involved individuals examining their
patterns of habitual thinking and then attempting to alter these negative thinking
habits to more constructive ones. Finally, relapse prevention was the central
theme of the sixth session. Trainees received instruction on a process designed to
prevent them from forgetting to practice the mental self-leadership techniques
learned when faced with a threatening situation. At the conclusion of each of the
training sessions, the employees were instructed to apply the skills that they
learned to situations on their job (specific application is one of the topics in each
training session). Additionally, throughout the training, the employees were
reminded frequently that they must practice these newly learned self-leadership
strategies to enjoy the full benefits of using such mental skills.

(continued)

The training was successful. An assessment of the employees following the training indicated that they liked the program; experienced enhanced mental performance; utilized the principles in their daily lives; demonstrated enhanced thoughts under simulated conditions; and that the training significantly improved trainees' job satisfaction, self-efficacy, and mood. Additionally, the assessment indicated that the training enhanced employees' bankruptcy perceptions. After the training, the employees viewed the bankruptcy situation at America West in a more opportunistic manner. In sum, we feel this example from America West shows that employees truly can be taught to lead themselves.

SOURCE: Adapted from C. P. Neck, "Mental Self-Leadership Training: Teaching Employees to Be Opportunity Thinkers" in H. Sims and C. Manz, *Company of Heroes: Unleashing The Power of Self-Leadership* (New York: Wiley, 1996): 103–104; and C. P. Neck and C. C. Manz, "Thought Self-Leadership: The Impact of Mental Strategies Training on Employee Cognition, Behavior, and Affect," *Journal of Organizational Behavior* 17 (1996): 445–467.

Some interesting applications of self-leadership strategies have been employed successfully by several managers and have been reported in some interesting research.[14] These applications involved managers in a variety of jobs in retailing, manufacturing, public service, and advertising, including line and staff positions. In the various cases reported, specific behaviors were identified (e.g., time spent on the phone, timely completion of expense forms, informing others when leaving the office) for improvement, appropriate to the individual manager involved.

The advertising manager of a newspaper, for example, was able to deal effectively with several behaviors he identified as needing improvement. One problem targeted was his tendency to leave the office without leaving word where he was going and when he would be back that day (if at all). A simple cueing strategy was used to solve the problem: A "checkout" board was placed on the office door, which he could not miss seeing when leaving. Magnetic disks on the board could be moved easily to indicate if he was out of the building, if he would return, and when.

Similarly, a problem he had in getting himself to fill out expense forms in a timely manner (neglected sometimes for several months) was eliminated by having a secretary place an appropriate form on his desk at an appropriate time of the day (in the evening just before he went home). He always tried to be back in the office just before leaving for home and usually did not have many demands placed on him at this time. Thus, he could complete this task easily when cued by the form on his desk to do so. In addition, a wall chart was placed on his wall for the purposes of self-observation. Soon the manager was filling out the form every day. The wall chart, which indicated this performance improvement, provided the occasion for self-reinforcement. Also, by properly filling out the expense forms, the manager received the added benefits of not incurring personal financial loss (from not being reimbursed for his expenses in a timely manner) and was able to get a more accurate picture of expenses in his department.

In another case, an assistant retail store manager identified a behavior she would like to improve: frequent visits to her boss, resulting in excessive dependence (her boss agreed that this was detracting from her effectiveness). To deal with the problem, she used a simple self-observation strategy—she would carry an index card on which she recorded the frequency of her visits, the type of information she wanted at the time, and what happened when she handled the problem herself rather than consulting her boss. Subsequently, the frequency of her visits was reduced drastically, and she and her boss were pleased with her performance.

In addition to these case studies, we have conducted considerable research on this topic for individuals in more traditional work environments and more contemporary participative and team-based environments.[5] We also have observed numerous instances that provide insight regarding self-management of managers. We have witnessed, as you probably have, many instances when managers have developed their own tailor-made self-leadership strategies to deal with behaviors that need improvement. We have seen countless managers use checklists to guide their daily behaviors. We have seen managers take coffee breaks after successfully completing important tasks or switch their attention to a more enjoyable activity as a reward for their accomplishment. We have seen managers turn routine tasks into a kind of game or competition to make their work more naturally rewarding. We also are familiar with managers who have visualized the potential rewards of successfully handling current challenges (recognition, promotion, or imagining the achievement of some of the dreams they have regarding their work).

Unfortunately, we also have seen managers mentally and physically beaten by the way they approached their work. One manager, for example, reported extreme worry associated with his work. His thoughts seemed always occupied by images of impending disaster on the job—failure, reprimand from his boss, humiliation resulting from poor performance, and even dismissal. The pressures associated with his job (most of which were apparently greatly exacerbated in his mind, he admitted) made him irritable at work and at home and dissatisfied with his job, and brought him significant physical problems. He reported difficulty in sleeping and exhibited excessive tension that was sometimes debilitating to the point of making him physically ill. The pattern of his physical and mental behavior may well be bringing him to other more serious problems, such as ulcers or perhaps worse: One of his associates had recently had his second heart attack, apparently brought on by "overpressing" at work.

We are also familiar with another manager who worked in the same organization. He, in contrast, was enthusiastic about his work and seemed to be well adjusted. He practiced several self-leadership strategies (he was especially sold on "time management" techniques) and was well organized, relying heavily on systematic analysis of business information. In particular, he had a strong sense of task completion. Until he achieved immediate goals, he was persistent in his work efforts. In many ways, he seemed like the model contemporary manager.

Unfortunately, this individual's strong sense of self-leadership did not extend to his impact on his environment or, more specifically, his immediate subordinates. His systematic approach to management was, frankly, not palatable to his subordinates. They preferred to operate using a "sense of the business" or intuition based on experience rather than to gather data and fill out reports systematically. Ultimately, the friction came to a head and the manager was squeezed out of the organization—despite a solid performance record.

The case of this manager illustrates once again the complexity of self-leadership. Indeed, we must recognize the importance of the indirect impact of our actions on our external world (e.g., the work environment), as well as the direct way we manage our own behavior and thoughts. Unfortunately, our work environment is often difficult to manage; for example, we have observed the frustrating plight of many managers attempting to maintain a consistent level of performance and motivation in the face of seemingly irrational organization roadblocks. We remember an instance when a customer wanted an odd table leaf owned by a large company—and the company wanted to get rid of the leaf that was taking up space. Unfortunately, the computer ticket that reported the style number, manufacturer, and other information for inventory purposes had become detached and lost. There was the customer, and there was the table leaf, but a manager in charge of the selling area could not for the life of him—despite numerous inquiries regarding appropriate procedures—figure out how to sell the leaf without breaking company policy for inventory-control purposes.

We also remember a manager who had been assigned, essentially, one and one-half jobs: his usual tasks in addition to the large bulk of what another individual had previously worked on full time. A few months later, computer reports revealed that the business was up 70 percent over the previous year. Despite these improved figures, he received little, if any, positive feedback from his superiors. On the other hand, a short time later when some inventory had been temporarily misplaced (by persons working for advertising and display without his knowledge and permission), he was vigorously chewed out by a vice president. Similarly, concern was expressed when financial indicators showed performance had dropped temporarily to a mere 40 percent, rather than 70 percent, ahead of the previous year. Fortunately, he was able to maintain his performance level and reasonably good morale by recognizing and reinforcing himself in the absence of external recognition.

Consider also the case of the manager who was considered somewhat ridiculous and was sometimes openly chided by peers because she refused to distort certain financial figures to make performance look better on paper than it was. This was a commonly accepted practice in the organization, despite the fact that to an outsider it would appear unethical. This manager's sense of ethics (her own personal standards) conflicted directly with those of her peers. To maintain the personal stand she believed in, she had to exercise self-leadership influence in excess of the external forces she faced.

Managers face difficult challenges. With significant pressures and often inhospitable external work environments (not to mention the difficulty involved in trying to manage one's self effectively), achieving personal effectiveness can be difficult. Although special problems such as managing time or controlling stress have received specific attention, managing one's day-to-day behavior has been largely neglected. This book is intended to be a significant first step in providing managers, and others, with practical tools for self-leadership. It represents a beginning step in dealing with challenges such as those discussed in this chapter.

Practicing Self Leadership in Russia: The Issue of Empowerment

—Carl F. Fey
Assistant Professor, Stockholm School of Economics
Associate Dean of Research, Stockholm School of Economics in Saint Petersburg

Every country has certain issues that require extra attention from leaders. In Russia, one of the most important and troubling issues for people trying to practice self-leadership is how to deal with empowerment, which is at the core of self-leadership. Historically, Russian firms have been hierarchical and had strong, powerful leaders who kept control of most decisions themselves and delegated little; this continues to be the norm in many firms even today. Thus, as the following examples will illustrate, now when some leaders (particularly in foreign firms) try to empower their employees in Russia as part of the self-leadership process, this poses challenges that are unlikely to occur to the same extent in the United States. However, effective empowerment can be achieved in Russia.

While Swedish multinational companies are now keen to create organizations with more empowerment, managers are discovering that creating empowerment takes time. As a manager at Ericsson Russia said, "We learned the hard way that you cannot just say 'now you are empowered.' Employees have to accept being empowered. It takes both a subordinate and a boss to follow empowerment for it to work." Many managers we have interviewed in Russia have stressed the importance of a gradual evolution to empowerment so that the system is effective and works well. Too much empowerment too soon can lead to chaos and an uncomfortable feeling for employees.

As an interesting case, consider the general director of the 300-person Russian subsidiary of Alfa Laval, a Swedish multinational firm that makes dairy equipment and district heating equipment, who would often delegate decision making to middle management. Despite the fact that he had delegated the authority to make decisions, the middle managers would come back repeatedly to get him to "decide" on an issue that officially had been passed down to middle management. The general manager found that the best course of action was to respond initially by asking for the pros and cons of different alternatives but, in the end, try to force middle managers to make the decision. The general manager thought that this was better than abruptly telling middle management that it was their job to decide. Over time, the middle managers slowly learned to act more empowered and make decisions delegated to them.

Under Communism, one was punished severely for mistakes, and little reward was given for good suggestions. The key goal under Communism was to meet production targets handed down from above. Developing innovative ways to produce more than the required target and then potentially falling short at some point in the future would result in later punishment and little current reward. This created an incentive for employees to want to just do what they were told to do and not think for themselves or exercise self-leadership. Further, because people were punished severely for mistakes, they always wanted their bosses to make decisions so that they were not responsible. This created a situation in which people did their job without concern for how it fit into the big picture.

Recently I was at a consulting factory in Russia and observed that a machine breakdown was causing a significant bottleneck. I inquired how long the machine had been broken and was told that it had been out of commission for 2 months. I asked the area supervisor what he had done about it, and he told me that he had reported that it was broken when the problem first occurred. The

(continued)

supervisor seemed confused when I asked him if he had done anything after that. Unfortunately, all too often in Russia, people do not practice self-leadership and act empowered; in this case, no one took responsibility for trying to get the machine fixed quickly. It is important to stress that despite the legacy just described, Russia has many talented, capable, and motivated people who when exposed to role models practicing self-leadership can adopt this style effectively over time. In fact, I would argue that human capital is the most undervalued resource in Russia. When you put Russians in the right environment, they can do extraordinary things.

One of Ericsson Russia's expatriate managers explains how he is trying to enact just such a transformation of leadership style at Ericsson Russia.

> Russians are used to having somebody deciding everything above them. . . . They have to learn by experience—eventually our managers will be very good because they are very capable people. They are not used to guiding and helping others. . . . It's the Swedish way of managing—giving guidance supervision and delegating and getting consensus. You have to convince people. Russians are more inclined just to decide, but then people further down in the organization don't work so hard for the success of the idea as much because they don't feel it is their idea. Further, you just don't have time to decide everything yourself as a manager.

Four important points shine consistently through these examples: (1) Russians are capable people when placed in the correct conditions; (2) empowerment can work in Russia over time with the appropriate role models and processes in place; (3) empowerment is a process, not an event—it takes time; and (4) both sides need to accept and understand empowerment for it to work effectively.

NONMANAGEMENT JOBS

Lower-level, hourly type jobs—the seemingly most unlikely focus for self-leadership application—have received perhaps the greatest attention. Recent growth in the adoption of self-managed or autonomous work teams in production/manufacturing plants and various other types of work settings (e.g., coal mines; warehouses; paper mills; and service organizations in insurance, financial services, and even psychiatric care) is the most striking example of this emphasis. The primary method we will use here to illustrate the need and potential of self-leadership methods for hourly workers is to draw upon examples from our personal experience and research. We have completed research projects in many self-managed team work systems across a wide variety of industries (manufacturing and service) and work settings. In particular, we will place special emphasis on nonmanagement jobs by contrasting the personal experiences of Charles Manz (CM) (the coauthor of this book) as a machine operator in a "traditionally managed" manufacturing plant some years ago. Manz was a college student who had obtained more recent observations from a research project conducted in a manufacturing plant based on a self-managed team work system.

The plants were similar in numerous ways: Both used assembly line technology, employed blue-collar workers with a relatively low level of education, and were even owned by the same corporation. A primary difference existed, however, regarding the way people were managed in the plant.

A common impression of blue-collar jobs in production/manufacturing plants is that they are monotonous, boring, and dehumanizing. CM's experience did not contradict this impression. The extent to which people in such work settings typically have been underutilized is especially striking. CM witnessed an interesting illustration of this tendency while working as a machine operator on a midnight shift. CM had been operating a lathe, as did several other workers around him, for several nights. On this particular evening, CM was approached by the foreman. He expressed in some heated words that CM was not producing enough output. Up to this time, CM had been attempting to work at about the same pace as the other workers, being sensitive to productivity norms that assured workers of not making each other look bad. The foreman's comments, however, apparently hit a raw nerve concerning CM's need for achievement—and he began working "like crazy." Soon CM's output was noticeably increased on the conveyer line that wound its way through his part of the plant. A short time later, the foreman approached CM again, this time grinning. "Wow, you're really going now. Good job," he remarked.

Meanwhile, another worker nearby had been observing all this. He was a man in his mid-thirties. He had always struck CM as a particularly bright individual (though not well educated), but not motivated. In fact, CM had learned recently that he would press the production counter lever on his lathe (CM later found out this was a common practice in the plant) to make it appear that his production was higher than it was. He moved slowly and looked lazy.

On this occasion, however, the coworker suddenly came to life. CM was awed by the controlled speed and smoothness of his motions. The coworker started producing "like hell," though with apparent lack of effort and fatigue. His face had come to life, as well, with determination and even pride. He apparently was trying to show the college punk a thing or two—and he did. CM felt rather awkward and inadequate in comparison.

The funny thing about the episode is that soon it seemed as if it had never happened. A couple of days later, CM had fallen back to a more restricted level of production, assisted by various subtle pressures from other workers. Meanwhile, the "super" lathe operator returned to his normal behavior, and he recaptured the dull, bored look on his face. He never produced the way he had that night during the remainder of CM's tenure in the plant.

Workers suffering from a severe lack of motivation are not found only in manufacturing plants; unfortunately, they are everywhere. Often the motivation that these workers possess is much more oriented to avoiding work than to doing it. For example, CM was familiar with one individual working in a warehouse who displayed an amazing aptitude in this regard. The creativity and effort he expended on avoiding work often exceeded that required to just go ahead and do the work. He enjoyed avoiding his work much more than doing it, so that's what he did.

Individuals such as this are not just lazy people without ambition. In fact, we have encountered many "work avoiders" who displayed obvious enthusiasm when they talked about their dreams of what they would *really* like to do. One factory worker CM knew related to him with excitement the dream he planned to fulfill some day: open a Disneyland type of park for African Americans. As he talked about it, the detail that he had worked out for his plan impressed CM—the idea sounded like it could work! Another, a warehouse worker, reported his ambition to own and operate his own ice-cream parlor. The energy and enthusiasm he displayed as he talked about his dream were in sharp contrast to the dull lack of motivation he displayed on his current job. Indeed, people such as these have a burning desire inside to put themselves into something they believe in. Unfortunately, when CM knew them they lacked the confidence and self-leadership capabilities to find a reasonable fit between their interests and their immediate and longer-term career efforts. They were wasting on their jobs.

One striking example of this sad state of affairs occurred on CM's last day of work on the midnight shift. CM had become good friends with most people on the shift and was given a warm and hearty good-bye from many people. One of the workers (we'll call him Ed), however, was being conspicuously aloof. Because CM had developed a particularly close tie with Ed and another worker on the shift, CM was surprised at his behavior. He seemed rather depressed and perhaps a bit angry for some reason. CM finally asked his other friend what the problem was. He explained that Ed was feeling down because CM was going back to college and he was stuck on a job he did not like. It seems that years earlier, Ed had chosen to work at the plant because the money was good, but he had always planned to get into some other more rewarding type of work. Now he was finally realizing that it was, perhaps, too late. He had become dependent on the money, and his youth had been largely spent; he had led himself into what he now saw as the trap of many unmotivated, demoralized American workers. This reality was dealing him a painful blow that evening. CM never saw Ed after he left, but he'll never forget the cold reality of the psychological defeat that showed on Ed's face that night.

It is little wonder to us that we have severe productivity problems in the United States when we see workers such as these. They derive no enjoyment from their work. Fortunately, it does not have to be that way. In fact, CM observed a situation in another manufacturing plant, this time as a researcher conducting a joint project with his colleague, Dr. Henry Sims, Jr., that supports this premise. What they saw was a sharp contrast to the examples related thus far. It was a plant that was organized on a self-managed team basis.[16] That is, production workers were provided with the autonomy and even the responsibility to do many things traditionally handled by managers (e.g., assigning group members to tasks, solving quality problems, and handling interpersonal problems between group members). Self-managed groups might be described as a step beyond the quality circles that have received so much attention because of their widespread use in Japan and extensive adoption in the United States. The important point for this discussion is that this plant, in contrast to the one CM had worked in, allowed and even encouraged blue-collar workers to exercise self-leadership.

Perhaps a few examples will serve to illustrate the point. One case observed involved a worker and his coordinator (in this plant, supervisors were referred to as *coordinators* because of the unique aspects of the work system). The worker was asking his coordinator how he should go about repairing a guardrail on a loading ramp. The coordinator's response was essentially a question: "How do you think you should do it?" The worker responded by stating what he thought the appropriate solution was and, consistent with the nature of the work system, proceeded to act on his solution. He also did it with conviction and commitment that probably wouldn't have been there if he had been complying with an order. This case is not especially remarkable itself, but multiply this case many times and you have a situation that can only be described as amazing by comparison to the usual atmosphere found in most production plants today.

Some of the observations were much more striking. They witnessed one instance, for example, in which a worker apparently saved the plant a great deal of money.[17] He left his workstation to test some production materials he suspected were defective. He proceeded to a laboratory area, where he performed a test that proved he was right. After quite a bit of commotion in the plant, corrections were made that might have saved the plant a day or more of production and thousands of dollars. This same worker stayed after his shift hours without pay to help make the necessary corrections.

Having both worked in settings with climates more consistent with typical impressions of production plants—where employees are placed in monotonous jobs that turn people into unmotivated "machines" who don't care about productivity or quality—Dr. Sims and CM were particularly amazed by instances such as these. They saw workers solve difficult technical and personal problems; they saw them volunteer to help complete difficult tasks without being told to do so; they heard them praise one another for work well done and provide negative feedback to fellow workers for not pulling their weight; they heard them refer to their work team's task responsibilities as "our business" and saw them talk to members of plant management (including the plant manager) as though they were equals. Most of all, they saw one of the best plants (and in many cases *the* best) in its product classification on many performance indicators measuring productivity, quality, safety, morale, turnover, and absenteeism.

The employees at the plant did not have the benefit of familiarity with the research and knowledge available regarding the systematic self-leadership strategies outlined in this book. Manz and Sims' research indicated, however, that they already were using many of these strategies without realizing they were doing so. The advantage they did have over workers in more traditional plants stemmed from their work environment, which provided the opportunity for them to use their innate abilities to lead themselves. This plant, we believe, represents just the tip of the iceberg in terms of what is possible. The primary stand of this book is that self-leadership can be used to improve one's personal effectiveness. It also can be used, however, to help others become more effective. The manager who is wise enough to provide an environment for workers to exercise more fully their self-leadership potential, for example, could reap substantial benefits on several bottom-line performance measures. In addition, by helping workers master self-leadership skills (such as those outlined in this book), significant benefits should result for the worker and the manager. All this calls for a new, more contemporary style of leadership—leadership that centers around the power of self-leadership.[18]

The tremendous potential of human beings to lead themselves to personal effectiveness is an expansive frontier just waiting to be explored. The examples related in this chapter are but a primitive glimpse of a few grains of the vast sands of self-leadership possibilities waiting to be tapped. Indeed, the ultimate journey is not the exploration of new lands or the outer regions of the cosmos; instead, it is the discovery of the tremendous unexplored regions of the human potential (the miracles) locked inside each one of us.

Notes

1. See, for example, Carl E. Thoresen and Michael J. Machoney, *Behavioral Self-Control* (New York: Holt, Rinehart and Winston, 1974); and Paul Karoly and Frederick H. Kanfer (eds.), *Self-Management and Behavior Change* (New York: Pergamon Press, 1982).

2. Alan E. Kazdin, "Effects of Covert Modeling and Model Reinforcement on Assertive Behavior," *Journal of Abnormal Psychology* 83 (1974): 240–252; and Alan E. Kazdin, "Effects of Covert Modeling, Multiple Models, and Model Reinforcement on Assertive Behavior," *Behavior Therapy* 7 (1976): 211–222.

3. For a comprehensive discussion of a plethora of research that examines the application of self-leadership techniques to a sport's setting, see C. P. Neck and C. C. Manz, "Thought Self-Leadership: The Influence of Self-Talk and Mental Imagery on Performance," *Journal of Organizational Behavior* 13 (1992): 681–699.

4. See T. K. Scanlon and M. W. Passer, "Sources of Competitive Stress in Young Female Athletes," *Journal of Sport Psychology* 1 (1979): 151–159; and T. K. Scanlon and M. W. Passer, "Factors Restored to Competitive Stress Among Male Youth Sport Participants," *Medicine and Science in Sports* 10 (1978): 276–281.

5. D. L. Feltz and D. M. Landers, "The Effects of Mental Practice on Motor Skill Learning and Performance: A Meta-Analysis," *Journal of Sport Psychology* 5 (1983): 25–57.

6. Maxwell Maltz, *Psycho-Cybernetics* (Upper Saddle River, NJ: Prentice Hall, 1960): 35–36.

7. Michael J. Mahoney, "Cognitive Skills and Athletic Performance" in P. C. Kendall and S. D. Hollan (eds.), *Cognitive-Behavioral Intervention: Theory, Research, and Procedures* (New York: Academic Press, 1979).

8. Ibid.

9. R. G. Ness and R. W. Patton, "The Effects of Beliefs on Maximum Weight Lifting Performance," *Cognitive Therapy and Research* 3, no. 2 (1979).

10. See, for example, Debra L. Feltz and Maureen R. Weiss, "Developing Efficacy Through Sport," *Journal of Physical Education, Recreation and Dance* (March 1982): 24–26, 36.

11. See C. P. Neck, H. M. Neck, and C. C. Manz, "Thought Self-Leadership: Mind Management for Entrepreneurs," *Journal of Developmental Entrepreneurship* 2 (1997): 25–36.

12. Charles C. Manz and Charles A. Snyder, "Entrepreneurial Self-Management or To Survive or Not to Survive, That Is the Question," *Management Review* (September 1983): 68–73.

13. Peter F. Drucker, *Managing for Results* (New York: Harper & Row, 1964).

14. Fred Luthans and Tim R. V. Davis, "Behavioral Self-Management—The Missing Link in Managerial Effectiveness," *Organizational Dynamics* (Summer 1979): 42–60.

15. See, for example, Charles C. Manz and Henry P. Sims, Jr., "Leading Workers to Lead Themselves: The External Leadership of Self-Managing Work Teams," *Administrative Science Quarterly* 32 (1987): 106–128.

16. For a good description of some of the unique aspects of this plant, see Henry P. Sims, Jr., and Charles C. Manz, "Conversations with Autonomous Work Groups," *National Productivity Review* (Summer 1982): 261–269.

17. Ibid.

18. See, for example, C. Manz and H. Sims, Jr., *Company of Heroes* (New York: Wiley, 1996); and Charles C. Manz and Henry P. Sims, Jr., *The New SuperLeadership: Leading Others to Lead Themselves* (San Francisco: Berrett-Koehler, 2001).

CHAPTER

The Destination

or Self-Leadership

> *What we call the beginning is often the end, And to make our end is to make a beginning. The end is where we start from.*
> — T. S. ELIOT

The primary ingredients of the self-leadership framework presented in this book have now been introduced. In addition, Chapter 8 presented some examples indicating how specific self-leadership techniques have been used in several different types of real-life situations. The purpose of this chapter is to present an integrative self-leadership framework combining those elements that have been suggested thus far. An illustrative case will be offered that is designed to exemplify how the various self-leadership elements might be combined into a comprehensive self-leadership framework to develop a new, more effective way of working and living in our complex and often troublesome world.

It has been a long journey, but the destination and a beginning are at hand. Read on to see the full form of our ultimate goal: self-leadership.

SELF-LEADERSHIP

To gain a fuller understanding of self-leadership and the various factors involved, it is important to describe an integrative framework. In essence, we have thus far been focusing on and examining the details of the various pieces of a larger self-leadership puzzle. At this point, we will examine how these pieces fit together to form the complete picture.

Figure 9-1 presents a diagram combining the key elements of self-leadership discussed in the previous chapters. The four major parts of the diagram correspond with the topics in Chapters 3, 4, 5, 6, and 7: strategies used primarily to alter our immediate physical world and to help us exercise control over ourselves, strategies for tapping the power of natural rewards, techniques for redesigning our psychological worlds, and tools to lead ourselves within a team setting. Note that consistent with Chapters 5 and 6, beliefs, imagined experiences, and self-talk are depicted as interacting factors that lead to the thought patterns that establish a unique psychological world for each of us.

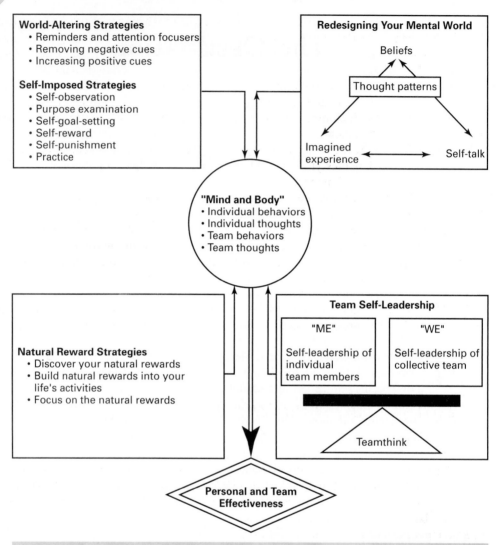

World-Altering Strategies
• Reminders and attention focusers
• Removing negative cues
• Increasing positive cues

Self-Imposed Strategies
• Self-observation
• Purpose examination
• Self-goal-setting
• Self-reward
• Self-punishment
• Practice

Redesigning Your Mental World

Beliefs

Thought patterns

Imagined experience ⟷ Self-talk

"Mind and Body"
• Individual behaviors
• Individual thoughts
• Team behaviors
• Team thoughts

Natural Reward Strategies
• Discover your natural rewards
• Build natural rewards into your life's activities
• Focus on the natural rewards

Team Self-Leadership

"ME"
Self-leadership of individual team members

"WE"
Self-leadership of collective team

Teamthink

Personal and Team Effectiveness

FIGURE 9-1   A Comprehensive Self-Leadership Framework

The diagram also illustrates that each of the four key dimensions to self-leadership influence and complement one another in forming a comprehensive framework.

The center of the diagram, "Mind and Body," is the ultimate focus of self-leadership—the primary concerns of self-leadership are our behaviors and thoughts, and how these affect our personal effectiveness (our success in achieving our goals as well as our satisfaction with our work, ourselves, and our lives) and our effectiveness as members of a team. The diagram points out that each of the four parts of self-leadership has an impact on our behaviors and thoughts, and ultimately on our personal and team effectiveness. The model also depicts the reciprocal influence (as depicted by the double arrow) between a person's psychological world and his or her corresponding thoughts and behaviors.

Figure 9-1 allows us to view the comprehensive systematic approach to self-leadership in its totality. A complex system of multiple variables is suggested, indicating that we have several points of departure in our undertaking to improve our self-leadership. Applying principles suggested by the various strategies that have been outlined also should contribute to improvements in the other approaches. For example, by effectively applying self-leadership techniques such as self-goal-setting and self-reward, indirect benefits including increased enjoyment of our work (natural rewards) and improved, more beneficial patterns of thought should be fostered. Ultimately, beneficial application of the various techniques should contribute to a changed, more effective and rewarding lifestyle and outlook. Ideally, this new pattern of self-leadership will be tailored to the unique values and needs of each of us.

In Chapter 8, examples were offered to illustrate how specific self-leadership strategies have been applied to deal with various challenges and problems. Although these examples are informative, their shortcoming is that they cannot adequately illustrate the comprehensive self-leadership system outlined in Figure 9-1. Consequently, we close this chapter with a fictitious case, inspired by our research and experience with self-leadership, designed to illustrate how a number of specific self-leadership strategies might combine to benefit a specific individual: one who, like you and us, is trying to cope effectively and enjoyably with the many challenges we face in our complex world. Such an excursion will, we hope, be instructive as well as entertaining.

A Tale of Self-Leadership

Tom Bigsby and Jennifer (Jen) Wilks have never met; nevertheless their lives display some amazing parallels. They both work for regionally based, medium-sized companies in middle-management positions. Each has a loving spouse and a son and a daughter, ages 9 and 11, respectively. They both live in a nice suburban home in a large metropolitan area. In countless ways, Tom's and Jen's situations are amazingly similar. The way they live their lives, however, differs like night and day.

A Day in the Life of Tom Bigsby

"What do you mean 'The budget is out of line'?" Tom blurted out angrily. "You guys are just great! You want my department to achieve miracles, and you won't even provide us with the resources we need."

Don Greenlaw, the vice president of financial control, scowled back at Tom. "We don't want excuses here—we want performance; and as for your budget, it is just plain too extravagant."

"If we didn't clamp down on unreasonable budget requests like this one, we would have everyone feeding at the troughs too long," chimed in Bob Harris, the division manager, with an obvious tone of superiority in his voice.

Tom felt the veins bulging in his neck. It was obvious to him that the members of the budget committee had their minds made up before the meeting even started and were basing their judgments on a narrow-minded, conservative stance as they always did. He had had it this time. He rose to his feet to vent his rage and . . .

"Honey, I wish you wouldn't gulp your food that way. You know the doctor said you need to learn to take things easier and relax."

"Never mind, Helen. I've got things on my mind," Tom snapped back. He leaned back stiffly into his chair a bit and let out a sigh. "This is going to be some day," he thought to himself miserably.

"Damn snow," Tom muttered as he scraped the ice off the windshield of his car. As he climbed in and started the engine, he felt symptoms of a nagging case of heartburn, apparently resulting from his hurried breakfast. Soon he was out on the expressway, on his way to work with the radio turned to the news, as usual. He occasionally commented sarcastically about "those incompetents in Washington" or complained about some other news issue as he weaved in and out of traffic in an attempt to hasten his drive to work. He did not notice the sunshine gleaming on the new-fallen snow that blanketed the trees, or the smiling snowman with hand raised in a gesture of friendly greeting next to a home visible from the road. Tom was deep in thought, recounting the problems he had faced the previous day and visualizing distasteful results of the budget meeting he was to have that afternoon.

After parking his car, Tom quickly entered the tall office building of the beautifully landscaped complex in which he worked, occasionally muttering a hurried hello with a forced smile to persons he encountered. Tom felt that many of the people working for his company seemed friendly, but he did not spend much time interacting on a personal basis. He felt the purpose of his job was clear—and that was to work. Personal conversation or interaction was not important, including that which occurred over lunch, which he frequently skipped.

Tom threw a quick "hello" at his secretary and a nearby colleague as he promptly entered his office, removing his coat and hat as he did. He heard, but hardly noticed, the rather stiff, proper responses to his greeting in the wake of his departure. Tom sighed as he looked around the room. He did not like his office because it was here that he faced and suffered through the burden of troublesome problems. Soon he was shuffling through a pile of paper on his desk, scarcely noticing that his secretary had brought him his usual cup of black coffee.

The next 2 hours were mostly a blur to Tom as he repeatedly shifted his focus from one task to another. He was frequently interrupted by phone calls and employees with problems—mostly minor ones. Several stacks of reports and files had been pushed to the far side of his desk—some had been there for several days—while he worked on the immediate problems before him. It seemed he never had time to think about or plan his actions.

Meanwhile, the snow continued to fall, and the view of the snow-blanketed countryside from his 12th-story window was breathtaking. A shimmering frozen lake was in the foreground and thick forests and rolling hills sat further away. Tom rarely looked up from his work, however, even when conversing on the phone. When he did have occasion to glimpse out the window, his thoughts were directed to potential problems with road conditions for his return trip home. "Damn winter," he muttered to himself.

At about 11:30 an employee in obvious distress entered Tom's office. "Mr. Bigsby, we're out of materials again," he complained, "and Supplies says there are none in stock."

"Damn!" said Tom to no one in particular. "I haven't had time to look at the supplies situation. I'll try to arrange for a rush order, although I haven't had much luck in the past trying to push things through. Maybe I can use possible cancellations in the future as leverage if they don't come through for us," said Tom, turning to the employee. "In the meantime, do what you can."

The employee left, frowning and obviously dissatisfied. At that moment, the phone rang again. "Hello," Tom heard himself say as he picked up the receiver.

"Tom, I'm in a jam," said the voice on the line. "Your estimated sales report is long overdue, and the production folks say they can't wait any longer—they need the information today. Have you been working on it, Tom?"

"Uh, yes," said Tom a bit anxiously as he reached for one of the piles at the outside of his desk.

"I've got to have it today, Tom. I wish you would try to plan ahead a little more," said the voice.

"OK!" said Tom in an angry tone and a bit too loud.

Tom worked through his lunch hour, as usual. He did not like working through lunch, but he felt the best way to get ahead in the company was to push hard. His intention this day was to get out the overdue sales projection report and the rush order on materials. He was distracted by several minor problems, however, and found he had made little headway by 2 P.M. Since the budget meeting was scheduled for 2:15, he began throwing some materials together.

Tom entered the meeting room in an uneasy, defensive frame of mind. He felt sure the budget committee intended to provide him with minimal support. His greetings to individuals present reflected this belief; his greetings were short and terse. The members of the budget committee responded in kind, and soon the atmosphere in the room was uncomfortably strained.

Tom delivered his presentation in about one hour and 15 minutes. Several times he noted inconsistencies in what he said. Also, several issues were raised that he had not anticipated. His already strained manner of presenting his case became even more strained as time passed. Each time he encountered an issue that he was not adequately prepared for, he tried to compensate by expressing his opinions especially emphatically, despite the obvious lack of substantive support for these views. In desperation, he tried to push his budget proposal through by sheer aggressiveness. Meanwhile, he found that he was continually prodding himself with negative internal thoughts such as "Why did you say that? Now you really opened a can of worms, you dummy!"

By the end of the presentation, Tom was noticeably exhausted and frazzled. The budget committee seemed to realize this because they were even a little gentle in the delivery of their negative feedback to Tom. In short, they told Tom he had not adequately thought through and documented his needs. They explained that they could not approve the budget in its current form, and recommended that he resubmit either a substantially reduced or a much better documented version in a week.

At this point, Tom was no longer hearing all that was being said. He had, in essence, joined what he saw as his opposition by lambasting himself on the inside with negative internal self-statements: "I blew it again . . . I never get anything right . . ."

"You don't seem to have a sense of direction in your department—no specific goals that you're working toward . . ." the budget committee continued.

"Maybe I'm not cut out to be a manager," thought Tom. "I just don't know what's wrong with me."

The meeting was over. Tom felt deflated, and the committee members seemed sorry and disturbed with what had transpired. One committee member with obvious good intentions singled Tom out privately as the others departed. "Tom, I've been in your shoes before. I know what you're feeling. I've found that going over my presentations ahead of time helps a lot. It can help in detecting problems and making adjustments before you do it for keeps. Also, you need to do a little thinking about the direction of your department. You need to spend some time planning."

"I don't have time to waste that way," Tom snapped back.

"Frankly, Tom, having to redo the budget is not going to save you much time either," the man responded with a smile that he intended to be friendly and reassuring.

Despite the individual's good intentions, Tom was irritated. He left the meeting room in a huff.

After a couple more disorganized, hurried hours spent back in his office, Tom left the building, his briefcase full of troublesome problems that needed his attention. It had been another difficult day that had gone just as badly as he had expected. The snow had continued to lightly blanket the landscape and was now sparkling under the bright-orange setting sun. Laughter could be heard as a small group of employees playfully exchanged snowballs in the parking lot. Tom didn't hear. "Damn snow," he muttered as he swept the windshield of his car.

A Day in the Life of Jennifer Wilks

Jen's presentation to the budget committee had gone extremely well. "I appreciate your input," Jen was saying to the committee, "and your responsiveness to new ideas." She felt good about the strong support she had been given resulting from her effective budget proposal presentation. She had done a good job in providing convincing documentation and a well-thought-out, logical proposal for her requests.

Jen felt a sense of satisfaction surge through her. She was impressed with the integrity and sincerity with which the meeting had been conducted. This was the kind of meeting Jen enjoyed—challenging her to refine her ideas, yet with an atmosphere of openness and flexibility.

Feeling exuberant, Jen rose to her feet to express her appreciation and . . .

"Would you like some more coffee, dear?" asked Chris, Jen's husband.

"Uh, yes. Would you pour it into my thermos please?" she answered.

"You really seem to be deep in thought this morning. What's on your mind?" asked Chris as he poured the coffee.

"It's this budget committee meeting today. I think it's really going to provide me with an opportunity to state my case for the department to those that can make a difference. I expect it to be challenging, but I'm ready. I'm looking forward to it," responded Jen.

Jen settled back in her chair. "This is going to be some day," she thought enthusiastically.

After clearing the snow off the windshield of her car, Jen paused to toss a couple of snowballs at a nearby tree before climbing in and starting the engine. "This weekend will be a good time to take the kids sledding," she thought to herself. She imagined the kids laughing as they wooshed down a snow-covered hill.

Jen turned on the radio as she pulled onto the expressway. A newscast was on, so she turned to a station that was playing some quiet music. She liked to start the day with music rather than with the often bad news that she sometimes found had a negative effect on her thinking early in the day. She would catch up with the newspaper and evening newscasts later on. After driving a few minutes through the scenic snow-covered landscape, Jen decided to get a little work done. She turned off the radio and proceeded to dictate a couple of memos to a tape recorder she had conveniently located next to her on the seat. She drove at a leisurely pace, sipping her coffee and enjoying the view.

When Jen reached her office complex, she felt relaxed and ready for the day. She strolled into her building, once again enjoying the snow-covered setting around her as she took some deep breaths of the clean, fresh air. Jen paused to deliver hearty greetings to fellow employees she passed. She enjoyed the people she worked with and found personal interactions to be a good source of information and ideas. Jen also realized that they helped establish important relationships that fostered cooperation when she needed assistance from others to get things done.

Jen stopped for a friendly chat with her assistant and a small group of colleagues who were conversing outside her office. After a short but pleasant and relaxed conversation, Jen entered her office. She smiled as she looked around the room that she had decorated (within a limited budget) to her personal tastes. Jen liked her office because it was here that she faced many stimulating challenges. She made a determined effort to keep her job enjoyable by working to mold it to her likes. She found there were many things to enjoy in her work if she looked for them—and she did.

Before beginning work on specific tasks, Jen took a notepad, eased back in her chair, and just thought for a bit while she savored a cup of coffee. Jen made a list of the more important activities that needed her attention during the day—"preparation for the budget meeting" she wrote on the pad, and she added a star next to her notation for emphasis. The next couple of hours were spent working on the more important items on her list. She spent a good portion of her time reviewing the presentation she had planned for the budget meeting. She even spent some time rehearsing, quietly, the more important points she would make while also picturing a positive response and desirable outcome of the meeting.

As usual, Jen's assistant held her calls, allowing only the most important ones to go through to her. Jen had worked out a routine some months back where she would spend the better part of her mornings working on her more important activities, including planning. She designated a 2-hour period after lunch as her "communication/troubleshooting" time. She spends this time discussing problems directly with employees and following up on phone calls. Employees know that only emergencies are to be brought to Jen's attention outside the 2-hour period she has set aside after lunch. At first, employees resisted this limited open-door policy a little, feeling a bit shut out. But soon they came to look at it as an expression of confidence in their abilities. It was amazing how many problems they were able to solve on their own after limited access to Jen had been established. On the other hand, they knew Jen's doors were always open in the early afternoon.

While working, Jen would pause every so often to look at some of the pictures on her walls (many beautiful, resort-type settings that she had either been to or wished to visit someday) or to gaze out the window. The snow was still falling outside, and the view of icy ponds and snow-covered trees from her 10th-story window looked to her like the most beautiful of Christmas cards come to life. She sometimes let her thoughts drift to a cup of hot chocolate in front of her blazing fireplace with one of her kids in her lap or some other pleasurable scene. She found that short breaks such as these helped keep her relaxed and refreshed.

A small plaque Jen had placed on her wall caught her attention. It read, "There is nothing so powerful as the human mind well maintained and purposefully set into motion." I need to do some more developmental reading, she thought as though answering the plaque.

A determined smile came over Jen's face as she gazed far off somewhere into the realm of possibility. Suddenly her attention snapped back to the present as she was struck by a powerful idea. She had been struggling for days to come up with a more efficient way to process work going through the department. At this moment a new, innovative approach was clear in her mind. She quickly reached for a pad of paper (as she often did when a new idea came to mind).

"This will save us time and money," she thought enthusiastically. (The idea would later prove to reap these desirable results for the department and would play an instrumental role in Jen's next promotion.)

About 11:30 an employee in obvious distress entered Jen's office. "Jen, the last shipment of materials we received is defective. We can't get any work done without materials."

"Call Frank Smith in Supplies," responded Jen in a concerned but controlled voice. "We have a couple days' worth of emergency materials in stock. In the meantime, I'll call Fred Harris and have him rush us an order. We have a good working relationship, and I know he'll come through for me. Also, Dave, would you and the others take some time to think through a strategy for dealing with this kind of problem in the future? Maybe some kind of sample inspection could be made when the materials first arrive to help us detect problems *before* we're under the gun. Or maybe some other precautionary measure could be taken. Let me know what you think is best."

The employee left looking less concerned and with a sense of responsibility in his stride. Things hadn't always worked out perfectly since Jen had become department manager, but the employees always knew where they stood and felt that they were a part of things. Jen certainly did not try to do everything herself or be involved in all decisions concerning the department. The look of confidence and determination frequently seen on her employees' faces reflected the sense of responsibility they had come to feel under Jen's guidance.

The remainder of Jen's morning went well. Just before lunch, she looked at her list of important things she wanted to work on during the day and noted then with a sense of satisfaction that she already had finished most of them. She had a leisurely lunch with two of the employees in her department. She tries to arrange to go out with a couple of members of the department twice a week, rotating who she goes with. Jen finds that the generally relaxed conversations away from the office are invaluable in keeping her abreast of the concerns of her workers and new developments in the organization. The lunches also foster good working relationships among Jen and members of the department.

After lunch, Jen handled employee concerns and returned phone calls during her open office hours. This time is often rather hectic, but Jen tries hard to handle one matter at a time and to keep calm. She had arranged to shorten her office hours a little this day so that she would have a chance to collect her thoughts and briefly review her budget proposal one more time before the meeting. She made a list of pending matters and calls she had not been able to make today to be made in her office hours the following day. She usually found 2 hours a day to be more than adequate, so she felt confident she would catch up within a few days.

After a brief review, Jen went to the meeting room early, feeling a little nervous, but mostly confident and prepared. She delivered a friendly greeting to each budget committee member individually. Jen was pleased to have the opportunity to make the planned direction and resource needs of her department known to those individuals who held the purse strings in her company. She wanted to make the most of the time she had with them.

Jen's presentation lasted approximately 1 hour. It went smoothly as planned—and Jen knew it. Even the issues raised by the committee were handled well. "I understand your concern about the increase in materials costs I've requested, and that's why I've prepared these charts," Jen was saying toward the end of the session. "As you can see, the expansion we've made in our product lines *as well as* increased materials costs make the request only a slight increase over last year."

"Yes, I see," responded Stan Jones, the vice president of financial control. "In that light, the request does seem very much in line."

"It appears you've done your homework, Jen—I like the innovative changes you're establishing in your department," added Harry Willis, the division manager, who obviously was pleased.

Jen's budget was approved as proposed, and perhaps even more importantly, she had established improved professional relationships with instrumental persons in her organization. She felt good about the support she had been given. Her most important approval, though, came from Jen herself. She was liberal in her self-praise. The meeting was significant; Jen had done well, and she let herself know it. "This is just the beginning," she thought. "I'm going to make things happen. I'm going to make a difference around here—I know I can do it."

After receiving some compliments from individual committee members, Jen returned to her office feeling good. She spent a couple more hours working and made progress on some pending tasks, though she was a bit distracted in her elation. She left the office that day with no work to do. She usually is able to finish what needs to be done (those matters that could not be delegated) at the office, so she rarely does much work at home—although she often comes up with creative ideas for her department during her leisure hours, which she writes down on pads she has located conveniently in her home. Many of these ideas save Jen a great deal of effort later. She was ready to celebrate this evening. Jen found herself singing a couple of times while she reviewed her successes of the day, and once again enjoyed the snow-covered landscape. She thought to herself, "I really love this job. I believe this job utilizes my strengths, and it allows me to make a difference in the lives of my colleagues and the organization. What a day," she thought, "what a day." ■

THE TALE IN PERSPECTIVE

The case you have just read represents an attempt to illustrate two divergent patterns of self-leadership under essentially identical conditions. Both individuals are trying hard. Their general pattern of living, however, is leading to different types of results. Simply put, Jen is exercising effective self-leadership à la this book—Tom is not. Jen is applying many of the strategies and techniques that have been suggested, and she is doing so in a way that is consistent with her own situation and personal makeup. She is controlling cues (having phone calls held and limiting office hours), for example. She also is monitoring her progress (self-observation) by using lists of pending tasks as a guide. Items on the list represent her goals for the day. Also, rehearsing her presentation apparently contributed significantly to her success at the budget meeting—the major challenge of her day.

A primary strength in Jen's approach is her overall constructive and positive orientation to thinking and behaving. For example, she is liberal in her use of self-rewards at the physical level (a good lunch after a hard morning of work, rewarding herself with rest breaks from time to time while she enjoys the pleasant pictures on her walls and the view out her window, planning to celebrate the day's success when she gets home) and at the mental level (positive self-statements, imagining desirable experiences in the future). Perhaps even more importantly, Jen tries to build in, focus on, and otherwise experience the natural rewards of her work itself (surrounding herself with pleasant pictures on her office walls, she works in a steady and controlled, rather than frantic, haphazard style, and she purposefully seeks out the enjoyable aspects of her job). Also, it seems that Jen from time to time performs a mental examination of her purpose in life (thinking to herself why she loves her job and the contribution she is making as a result of her job).

Finally, and perhaps most importantly of all, Jen has adopted a desirable pattern of thinking. She has developed the ability to see through the often obstacle-laden exterior of challenges and to be especially responsive to the opportunities that are enveloped within. Her orientation is to strive to achieve further advances and progress rather than to flounder and give in to formidable problems. Her actions are controlled and well thought out, reflecting recognition of the obstacles that do exist. Her course of action, however, is founded more on advancing toward existing opportunities rather than retreating from obstacles. Jen has indeed established a positive world, psychologically and physically (e.g., through her actions toward others, she has won their support when she needs it), in the way she lives her life.

Tom's mode of living reflects to a large degree an opposite pattern of self-leadership. Tom does not manage his behavior through the use of self-leadership strategies. Instead, he works in a disorganized, haphazard manner; in addition, he takes a basically negative, destructive stance toward his work. He focuses on the distasteful aspects of his job and keys his efforts primarily on the immediate obstacles he faces. Tom expects his work experiences and outcomes to be unpleasant—and so they are. What little time he *does* spend thinking about positive aspects of his job centers on future promotions or pay raises, and not on what he does. He has created a negative world for himself through his thoughts and his actions (e.g., he does not behave in a manner that helps ensure that he will have the support of others when he needs it). Tom has a self-leadership problem that will likely preclude his achieving personal and professional effectiveness unless he makes some major changes.

Do either of these two fictitious characters remind you of yourself? Perhaps you see a little of both Tom and Jen in you when you gaze into the mirror. The point is, you *do* have choices. These include the way you choose to think about things and the way you choose to behave. This book offers a framework to help you choose intelligently and act on your choices wisely and efficiently.

Another type of fictitious character could have been developed—one who does not try at all or, in essence, one who does not care about personal effectiveness. I'm assuming, however, that those who would read a book on self-leadership *do* care and *do* want to succeed (according to their own standards). Consequently, the framework that has been presented is designed to provide insight into the choices you have concerning how you lead yourself to get more out of the effort you exert and the types of overall self-leadership patterns you can choose to establish for your life. If you are going to spend the effort to work and live, why not spend it wisely? Greater awareness and competence in applying the varied tools of self-leadership can be a powerful source of personal effectiveness. How are you spending your life? Are you moving ahead to benefit from the abundant opportunities that lie before you, or are you forever surrendering to obstacles along the way? The pursuit of self-leadership may well be the ultimate journey into yourself and your life. The destination is within your reach if you choose it to be.

Fitness and Self-Leadership[1]

10

Physical fitness is the basis for all other forms of excellence.
—JOHN F. KENNEDY

D uring our executive training and when teaching at our universities on the topic of self-leadership since the previous edition of this book was released, we realized that we were not completely "preaching what we practice." In other words, we truly believe that our physical fitness level plays an important role in determining our effectiveness in all aspects of our lives and that self-leadership strategies can help us obtain the fitness levels we desire. For example, Christopher Neck has run 12 marathons and runs almost every day. He recently completed a run of more than 30 miles, and he follows a strict diet. Charles Manz also does aerobic exercise daily, does strength training, watches what he eats, and practices meditation and Tai Chi. We both rely on a variety of self-leadership strategies (self-goal-setting, self-reward, cueing strategies, self-talk, mental imagery, etc.) to help us maintain our fitness activities. In fact, we have found that self-leadership contributes to good fitness habits, and good fitness enables us to be more personally effective in our work and lives. However, the previous editions of this book did not address the fitness aspect of self-leadership. Hence, this chapter was written to correct that omission. It is important to note that the focus of this chapter is on executives, but the lessons apply to all individuals, especially those who live hectic lives with busy schedules—which probably describes most people.

WHAT EXECUTIVES SAY ABOUT THE IMPORTANCE OF FITNESS

There's no question that people who are fit are more productive;
they enjoy their work more and accomplish more.
—DR. JEROME ZUCKERMAN
EXERCISE PHYSIOLOGIST

The job of the executive has become more intense over the last decade. A profusion of demands confronts them—especially physical ones. The global economic thrust of many businesses today has increased the amount of travel required by CEOs to develop and maintain an international presence for their companies. Another major physical demand is created by the stress related to being responsible for many people, their welfare, and the success of the company. Endless meetings and extremely long working hours are par for the course for executives. Executives who enjoy optimal fitness—that is, the ability to accomplish life's activities without undue fatigue—will be able to handle these demands more constructively and thus perform better in their daily tasks.

Indeed, data from personal interviews and related research support this fitness/performance relationship.[2] For example, Michael Mangum, president of The Mangum Group, a construction firm, states:

> I do believe fitness impacts my job. I usually exercise during the middle of the day—say, 1 to 4 P.M. or so. I find that my energy level is much enhanced when I return from a workout. Further, I find that because I choose to go during the day, my thoughts tend toward work while exercising. I have some of my most creative thoughts when working out.

Judith Kaplan had a similar perspective while she served as CEO of Action Products International, an educational toy manufacturer.

> I never felt better, physically and mentally, than when I was exercising regularly three times a week. I could still work harder, and instead of collapsing at the end of the day, I'd still feel good.

Likewise, Tom Monaghan, the founder of Domino's Pizza and current chairman of The Mater Christi Foundation, says:

> Since I have been exercising regularly and eating right, I have had more energy and a better self-image. Fitness and exercise also have helped me develop good disciplinary habits, which carries over to good business habits.

James Harris, director of Pro Personnel for the NFL's Baltimore Ravens, has a similar perspective.

> I believe fitness can enhance your concentration and endurance to perform the task at hand. Physical conditioning gives you confidence and energy to achieve.

Finally, Carol Cone, president of Cone Communications, also believes that fitness can enhance executive performance.

> I must make 50 to 100 decisions a day, and it's important to have the same clarity of thinking at 7 or 8 o'clock at night as at 7 or 8 o'clock in the morning.

THE IMPACT OF FITNESS ON JOB PERFORMANCE

Various studies show that fitness promotes job performance. For instance, commercial real estate stockbrokers who participated in an aerobics training program (walking and/or running once a day, three times a week, for 12 weeks) earned larger sales commissions during and subsequent to the training program than brokers who did not participate in the exercise program. Also, workers from a hospital equipment firm who participated in a similar aerobics training program (walking, running, swimming, and/or bicycling once a day, four times a week, for 24 weeks) enjoyed greater productivity and job satisfaction than workers who did not participate in the fitness program.[3]

In addition, a variety of studies support the relationship between fitness and mental performance, especially for individuals within the age ranges of many executives. For example, one study of 56 college professors revealed that physically active people process data faster and experience a slower decline in information processing speed than inactive people as they age. Similarly, the findings from a study of postal workers from 18 to 62 years of age suggested that older (43 to 62 years of age), less fit individuals consistently underperformed older, more fit people and underperformed younger individuals (18 to 30 years old) on mental tasks involving information processing.

A superabundance of other benefits also are related to being fit. Individuals who are fit are less likely to become obese, and are more likely to possess higher levels of energy and enjoy enhanced feelings of well-being.[4] Further studies have shown that fit individuals (those who participate in aerobic activity) tend to enjoy various psychological outcomes as well, including a reduction in anxiety, depression, tension, and stress.[5] In fact, Ken Resse, former executive vice president at Tenneco Incorporated, utilized exercise to help him cope with the pressures of being a top executive.

> [There's] no question my exercise program has helped me cope with stress. If it starts to build up, I just go out and run like hell. I'm a morning runner, and that sets the tone for the whole day. By the time I get to the office, I'm relaxed.[6]

Physiological benefits of individuals engaged in fitness programs also have been documented. The findings in one study revealed improvements in cardiovascular function and strength, as well as reductions in body fat and weight, for 66 men engaged in a 2-year exercise program located within the corporate headquarters. A study led by Dr. Dean Ornish showed that lifestyle changes that include improved diet and exercise habits can reverse the atherosclerotic changes of coronary heart disease and unblock arteries enough to avoid surgery. Finally, it has been estimated that 35 percent of cancers, the second leading cause of death in the United States, are related to diet.[7] In fact, a growing body of epidemiological evidence correlates diet with the incidence of cancer, particularly cancers of the esophagus, breast, prostate, and colon.[8]

Additionally, solid evidence shows that physically fit people live longer. A recent study published in the *New England Journal of Medicine* of more than 1 million adults during a 14-year-period confirmed that being overweight shortens a person's life. Additionally, several landmark studies at The Cooper Institute for Aerobics Research in Dallas have investigated the association between fitness and death. One of these seminal research projects investigated the relationship between fitness levels and the risk of dying in more than 10,000 men and 3,000 women. The study revealed that men and women with low levels of physical fitness had more than twice the mortality rate of persons with even a moderate level of physical fitness. Fitness in this case helped individuals overcome all causes of mortality, including diabetes, cancer, and heart disease.[9]

The major finding from this study and others—that physical fitness can prolong one's life—has tremendous significance for organizations and executives. The fitness level of their executives is something that companies need to consider in relation to the potential success of the company. An illness or the death of a top executive can have far-reaching consequences for an organization. Dr. Jerrold Post, coauthor of *When Illness Strikes the Leader*, states:

> In a company where you have an entrepreneurial leader who is so identified with the company, that kind of event [death or serious illness of a key executive] will strike at the core of its corporate identity.[10]

To put it briefly, executive fitness is not only personally important to executives themselves, but also to all the constituents of the executive's organization. The economic effects of cardiovascular disease (which research shows can be related to poor fitness habits) amounted to an estimated $286.5 billion in 1999.[11] According to the U.S. Department of Health and Human Services, such losses affect employer and employee alike "in lost workdays and wages, lost productivity, increased health care costs, and lowered morale."[12] Further, our claim is reinforced by Bob Jeffrey, president of the North America division of J. Walter Thompson advertising agency. Mr. Thompson sees the value of fitness to his company. His employees can "work out and relax in a 'de-stress room,' get free massages and yoga or nutrition lessons, join a company sports team, and consult with a personal trainer." As Mr. Thompson remarks:

> We're [the company] totally dependent on the ideas and talent of our people, so we have to help them feel great about themselves.[13]

Executive Fitness Behaviors at a Glance

In light of the information about the benefits of physical fitness, the question arises, If fitness is so important, how many executives are doing something to optimize their fitness levels? According to various accounts, many executives are indeed placing a priority on their physical fitness. A survey of executives from the top 3,000 U.S. companies (identified from Fortune 500, the Inc. 100, the Venture Fast Track 100, and Dun's List of Large and Small Companies) revealed that two-thirds of the executives surveyed exercise at least three times weekly, with more than 90 percent of that group using aerobic exercise as the cornerstone of their workouts. Additionally, this survey indicated that 90 percent of the executives want to improve their physical condition within the next 5 years. Finally, more than 90 percent reported being careful about their diet, 81 percent had a complete physical exam within the previous 2 years, and only 10 percent of the executives smoke (compared with the national average of more than 25 percent).[14]

Earlier, we presented some examples of executives who rank fitness as an important aspect of their lives. The following, based on examples gathered by the authors or that have been documented elsewhere, are some more brief descriptions of fitness used by current executives to enhance their abilities to lead their organizations.[15]

- Dina Gartland, a partner at age 31 at the geotechnical firm Leighton & Associates, is out of bed at 5 A.M. to train for 3 hours as a triathelete before starting a long workday.
- Dr. Thomas Frist, Jr., chairman and CEO of Columbia/HCA Healthcare, uses time between business flights to jog around airports or nearby cities.
- Charles O. Rossotti, commissioner of the Internal Revenue Service, jogs 5 miles a day.
- Julian C. Day, chief financial officer for Sears, Roebuck & Company, runs half marathons and surfs.

Despite these statistics and anecdotes that suggest that executives are prioritizing fitness in their lives, room for improvement still exists. A primary concern is that executives who are dedicated to fitness might be basing their exercise and diet routines on obsolete or incomplete data; that is, they are following the fitness fad of the month or outdated training and nutritional folklore.[16]

EXERCISE AND DIET: THE KEYS TO FITNESS

In their *Academy of Management Executive* article, "The Fit Executive: Exercise and Diet Guidelines for Enhancing Performance," Drs. Christopher Neck and Kenneth Cooper attempted to correct this misinformation on fitness as they outlined the exercise and diet-related prescriptions that would help executives achieve the optimal levels of fitness necessary for superior performance. In short, they argue that endurance, strength, and flexibility should be the focal points of an effective exercise program. Further, they suggest that adults should complete 30 minutes of moderate exercise per day.

What exactly is moderate exercise? Moderate exercise can be labeled as lower-intensity exercise. In short, this is exercising at one's target heart rate, which is the scientifically established higher-than-normal but less-than-maximum rate that allows executives to improve their endurance. To determine your personal target heart rate, subtract your age from 220 to get your predicted maximal heart rate. Then take 65 percent and 80 percent of that figure to obtain your target heart rate. For example, a 40 year old would have a predicted maximal heart rate of 220 minus 40, or 180. Multiplying that figure by 0.65 and by 0.80 produces a target heart rate range for endurance exercise of 117 to 144 heartbeats per minute.

When focusing on one's diet, Neck and Cooper suggest that an adult diet should consist of the following.

- No more than 20 to 25 percent of daily calories should come from fat.
- Of the 20 to 25 percent of daily calories from fat, it is recommended that most of this fat intake should consist of monounsaturated and polyunsaturated fat, but NOT saturated fat.
- About 50 to 70 percent of calories should come from complex carbohydrates, such as fruits, vegetables, legumes, and whole grain products—not from candies, desserts, or simple sugars, which are classified as simple carbohydrates.
- About 10 to 20 percent of calories each day should be from protein sources such as fish, poultry, and lean meats.

Did You Know?
The following is a list of the calorie content of some foods found at popular restaurants.

Cheese fries with ranch dressing	3,010
Fried whole onion with dipping sauce	2,130
Orange beef	1,770

(continued)

A large movie theater popcorn with butter	1,640
Kung Pao chicken	1,620
Sweet and sour pork	1,610
General Tso's chicken	1,600
The Cheesecake Factory Carrot Cake	1,560
Fettuccine Alfredo	1,500
House fried rice	1,480

NOTE: The average person needs about 2,000 to 2,500 calories per day.
SOURCE: Center for Science in the Public Interest

SELF-LEADERSHIP, FITNESS, AND PERSONAL EFFECTIVENESS

*For most of us, health will depend not on who we are, but on how we live.
The body you have at 20 depends on your genes, but the body you have at
40, 60, or 80 is the body you deserve, the body that reflects your behavior.*
—HARVEY B. SIMON, M.D.,
STAYING WELL

It is tough to motivate ourselves to exercise. Given our jobs, families, and other obligations, it is not difficult to talk ourselves out of going for that run or heading to the gym. It is much easier to grab fast food than to plan a healthy meal. The question is, How can you motivate yourself to stay fit, to exercise most days of the week, and to watch what you eat? The answer to this question lies in the concept of self-leadership. Next, we will discuss briefly how some of the self-leadership strategies outlined in the previous chapters can help you become more fit and thus more healthy and productive.

Self-Observation and Evaluation

Recall that self-observation and evaluation involve determining when, why, and under what conditions you exhibit certain behaviors. For example, if you feel you are not accomplishing enough each day (e.g., getting your workouts done) because of wasted time, you can study the distractions you experience. If you discover that the TV sucks you in when you might otherwise be exercising, then you can remove the TV, or you could put a treadmill in the TV room so you can exercise while you watch. Are you failing to stick to an optimal diet? Perhaps by observing yourself, you will notice that you primarily eat inappropriately when dining out. If so, perhaps by limiting the number of times you go to restaurants during the week, you can better achieve your fitness goals.

Removing Negative Cues

One strategy that can be used to eliminate our fitness-related behaviors that we don't like is to eliminate cues that lead to these behaviors. For example, if we want to cut down on our consumption of sweets, we can remove the candy dish from the coffee table. Similarly, the TV in the previous example is serving as a negative cue. If we are dis-

turbed about excessive time spent watching television (and the effect it is
our exercise activity) and we don't want to remove it completely, we can mov
set to another less-frequently used room.

We are surrounded by physical cues that tend to encourage certain behaviors. If
can identify the things that encourage our undesired behaviors, we can either remove
or alter them. In addition, we can remove ourselves from their presence. For example,
if we want to eat a diet that follows the guidelines specified earlier in this chapter, then
it would be a good idea to eliminate cookies from the pantry and high-fat ice cream
from the freezer. In fact, we can plan the furnishings and other features of the rooms in
our homes with healthy, constructive living in mind. Similarly, we can design our work-
space to eliminate cues to destructive, unproductive behavior.

Increasing Positive Cues

Cues also can serve as a positive part of our self-leadership practices. We can use physical
objects to remind us of, or to focus our attention on, things we need to do. President
George W. Bush relies on this self-leadership strategy when he travels by making sure
exercise equipment is located in his hotel room. Having the equipment in his room serves
as a reminder and focuses his attention on his need to exercise when he travels. Other
examples might include a clearly displayed sign on our refrigerator that reminds us to eat
a healthy, well-balanced diet or an inspiring picture on one of our walls displaying an athlete performing well in a physical sport in which we engage such as running or biking.

Self-Goal Setting

One especially effective way to help you lead yourself to perform challenging behaviors (e.g., exercising and eating right) is to set personal goals. For example, you could
set a goal of running a 10k race or a marathon, or taking a substantial hike. Such
longer-term goals help create the context for setting shorter-term goals that can help us
maintain fitness on a daily basis.

Self-set goals need to address long-range pursuits and short-run objectives along
the way. If we decide on a long-range goal of losing 50 pounds, we need to accomplish
many shorter-range goals, such as exercising for 30 minutes 5 days a week. The shorter-
range goals allow a sense of accomplishment on a smaller scale on the way to achieving
long-range goals. This process takes effort, and although our goals are likely to change
over time, it is important that we have current goals for our immediate efforts.

Finding Natural Rewards

Finding natural rewards in the tasks that we do is necessary to motivate us to exercise
and eat properly. An important part of self-leadership is based on relying on the natural motivation derived from activities that are naturally rewarding to do because they
make us feel more competent and self-controlling. An important lesson for becoming
and staying fit is this: Fitness activities you choose should be those you like to do and
are reasonably good at doing.

Purpose Development

In order to motivate yourself to exercise and eat appropriately on a daily basis, you have
to decide that it is important to you. If it is, then you need to make exercise a priority in
your life and pursue it with a sense of purpose. For instance, the president of the United

Bush, practices this self-leadership strategy of "purpose develop-
[th]at time for exercise be set aside each day (preferably at lunchtime)
[in] his busy schedule. The importance that the president places on fit-
[ness is shown by] the fact that he schedules exercise into his workday. As Bush says:

[Reporters wh]o had looked at my calendar noticed that I had about an hour-
[long block of free time each] day. I said, that is because I exercise every day. They asked if
[this was an indica]tion that I do not work very hard. I said, no, it is an indication
that I prioritize exercise. I told them [reporters] that I have given some of the
greatest speeches of my life while running . . . Running is therapy, running is a
chance to be alone, a chance to think . . . Running is an opportunity to be out-
doors in fresh air. Running is a wholesome and important experience for me.

Mental Imagery

Your mind can have a big impact on whether or not you achieve your goals—including
your fitness goals. In short, if you think you can become fit, you can. Conversely, if you
think you are too old, too busy, or too tired to maintain a fitness program, then you are!

Assume that you and a colleague have read the material in this book and have
agreed to begin a fitness program in order to make you more fit individuals and thus
more personally effective in your work and life. Suppose you picture in your mind
becoming frustrated with your workout program because you keep finding excuses to
skip your workout and not eat correctly, and eventually you give up on your fitness
program. You feel humiliated. This imagined experience could lead to lack of confidence and thus poor performance when you do begin your fitness program. Suppose
your colleague imagines a positive experience (losing weight, feeling more energized)
that results in enormous praise from coworkers and clients. This executive would likely
possess a higher level of self-confidence before starting the fitness program and probably will enjoy this imagined success. Mental imagery can help or deter you from
becoming fit. It depends on which picture you choose to create in your mind.

Self-Talk

If you currently are having problems getting to the gym and eating the right types of
foods, it could be related to what you are saying to yourself.

For example, think for a moment. Have you ever told yourself any of the following?

- I don't have the talent.
- I don't feel like working out today.
- I hate to exercise.
- I don't have enough time to go running today.
- I've eaten two cookies so I might as well eat the whole bag.
- Running on a treadmill is boring.
- If I don't order dessert like everyone else, I'm going to look like a wimp.

If you are like most of us, you have told yourself negative things similar to these
examples. These negative types of self-talk reduce your energy, your self-confidence,
and your happiness; they also prevent you from achieving your fitness goals and feeling

good about yourself. If you tell yourself you won't have a good day, you won't. If you tell yourself you can't lose weight, you won't. If you tell yourself that you don't enjoy working out, you won't. It is that simple. On the other hand, if you purposely choose positive self-statements (e.g., "This may be challenging, but I can do it and I will be healthier, feel better, and be more confident as a result), you can improve your self-leadership of your fitness activities significantly.

Beliefs

Recall the categories of dysfunctional thinking outlined in Chapter 5 (e.g., extreme thinking, mind reading, etc.). Then, imagine that an executive attempts to eat in a more healthy manner but ends up gaining weight after 2 weeks of this new nutritional program (due to too much late-night snacking). The executive thinks, "I am a failure. I'll never be able to get fit."

This scenario presents an example of dysfunctional thinking based on the distorted belief of "extreme thinking," which, as stated earlier, refers to an individual's tendency to evaluate a personal situation in extreme black or white categories. The executive is not thinking that some of the most fit managers failed in some early attempts to start a fitness program. The person is instead evaluating personal qualities in extreme black or white categories.

To alter this destructive belief, the executive must identify the dysfunction and then change the underlying thoughts so that they are more rational and constructive. The person can challenge private thoughts of being a complete failure and revise those beliefs by thinking "Some of the most healthy and fit people have failed in attempts to lose weight and exercise more. I shall learn from this mistake. It's not the end of the world; I will do better next time."

To summarize this discussion on fitness and how self-leadership strategies can help you achieve optimal fitness levels (and the related benefits), see the "self-leadership/fitness" framework in Figure 10-1. In short, self-leadership can help you increase your fitness, which in turn will result in a plethora of benefits to you as well as to your organization.

Self-Leadership and the Father of Fitness Dr. Kenneth H. Cooper

—T. L. (Tedd) Mitchell, M.D., Cooper Clinic,
and Emmet C. (Tom) Thompson II, D.SL., M.S.

It is easier to maintain good health through proper exercise, diet, and emotional balance than to regain it once it is lost.

—Kenneth H. Cooper, M.D.

In 1970, Dr. Kenneth H. Cooper resigned as a lieutenant colonel from a 13-year career in the U.S. Air Force medical corps in order to open a medical clinic and research center. As a result, Dr. Cooper was able to devote all of his time to studying the relationship of exercise to health and longevity.

(*continued*)

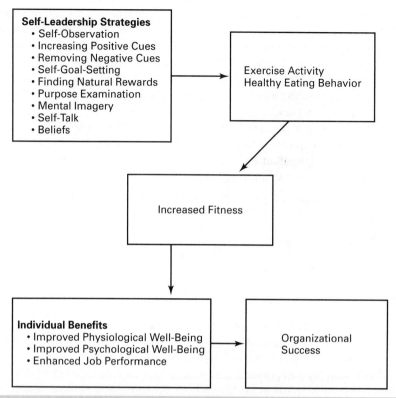

FIGURE 10-1   Self-Leadership/Fitness Framework Model

The Cooper Aerobics Center has grown from a one-man office in a shopping center to a 30-acre campus that includes a world-class fitness center with more than 3,000 members; a state-of-the-art clinic with a patient register of more than 70,000 and a staff of 18 physicians; a 62-room, colonial-style guest lodge and conference center; and a research institute with the largest computerized exercise database on record (e.g., approximately 350,000 person years of data). Dr. Cooper is recognized through his writings and research as the father of the physical fitness movement. Today, in his early 70s, Dr. Cooper still leads the Aerobics Center as president and chief executive officer.

Information obtained in an interview with Dr. Cooper clearly indicates that self-leadership is a key to his career success. For example, self-goal-setting and purpose examination are important self-leadership tactics practiced by Dr. Cooper to achieve personal, fitness, and career success. When Dr. Cooper was asked how he achieved so much, he was quick to point out that maintaining a daily routine was his first goal. By achieving this initial goal, Dr. Cooper reasons that all other goals are achievable. The following outlines a typical day in the life of the Father of Fitness.

I start my day with prayer and Bible study. My staff knows that that is my quiet time, and I do not want interruptions. In addition, I have my prayer list that I refer to daily. When I finish my day, I exercise. If I cannot exercise before I go home, I will walk approximately 2 miles at 10 o'clock at night. That combination of spiritual and physical discipline is one reason I am still functioning efficiently at almost 70 years of age when many of my colleagues who graduated from medical school when I did have expired. A third have retired. Less than a third of us are still practicing medicine. Here I am heading up a large organization with ever-increasing administrative responsibilities.

Obviously, staying fit is important to Dr. Cooper's success. His exercise program is as follows.

Walking: 5 to 6 days per week. 3 miles at 13 minutes per mile or jogging 3 miles at 10 minutes per mile or walk/jog 3 miles at 11 minutes per mile (ave.)

Weights: Twice a week. Consisting of 5 exercises at 65% capacity. 12 to 15 repetitions for approximately 20 minutes duration total.

Stretching: Twice a week for 3 to 5 minutes.

The importance of an individual having a purpose is fundamental to self-leadership. Indeed, having a purpose is a catalyst for achieving happiness, productivity, and organizing life. Dr. Cooper's purpose has been to provide a medical practice that is built upon his own personal core values. This internalization of values has provided Dr. Cooper with passion for his purpose. By combining purpose with a passion, Dr. Cooper created a force that helped him achieve his goals. Figure 10-2 outlines what Dr. Cooper views as his core values, as well as those of the Cooper Clinic.

FIGURE 10-2 Cooper's Core Values

Compassion: We have compassion for our patients and each other. Our actions show we care. We express concern and respect for our patients.

Credibility: Our physicians give sound medical advice based on facts. We strive to stay abreast of the latest medical research. We use new technology, materials, programs, and procedures that enable us to offer first-class care.

Commitment: We go the extra mile for our patients. Through teamwork, we are committed to exceed our patient's expectations and raise our levels of performance. We reward our staff who demonstrate their commitment.

Dedication: We focus our attention on our patient's needs. We continue to raise the standards of our services.

Honesty and Integrity: We conduct our evaluations with the care and thoroughness necessary to ensure the collection of accurate data. We address our challenges openly with concern for the best solutions. We are accessible to our patients. We return phone calls and answer correspondence promptly.

Outwardly Focused: Our patients are the reason for our business. We closely monitor what our peers are doing to enhance our ability to remain the world leaders in preventative medicine.

By setting goals and by finding and fulfilling his purpose, Dr. Kenneth H. Cooper has achieved optimal levels of professional and fitness goals and thus is a terrific example of someone who has attained the status of a master self-leader.

Notes

1. Much of the material in this chapter has been adapted and inspired from C. P. Neck and K. H. Cooper, "The Fit Executive: Exercise and Diet Guidelines for Enhanced Performance," *Academy of Management Executive* 14, no. 2 (2000): 72–83; and C. P. Neck, T. L. Mitchell, C. C. Manz, K. H. Cooper, and E. C. Thompson, "Fit to Lead: Is Fitness the Key to Effective Executive Leadership?", *Journal of Managerial Psychology* 15, no. 8 (2000): 833–840. Before embarking on any exercise and/or nutritional program, readers should obtain medical clearance from a qualified physician.

2. The source for the quotations by Mr. Mangum, Mr. Monaghan, and Mr. Harris was personal interviews conducted by the first author on February 26, 1999 (Mr. Mangum); March 23, 1999 (Mr. Monaghan); and March 15, 1999 (Mr. Harris). The quotes by Ms. Kaplan and Ms. Cone appeared in J. M. Rippe, "CEO Fitness: The Performance Plus," *Psychology Today* 23, no. 5 (1989): 50–54.

3. For more information about these studies and others that examine the fitness/performance relationship, see R. J. Shephard, "Do Work-Site Exercise and Health Programs Work?", *The Physician and Sports Medicine* 27 (1999): 48–72; D. R. Frew and N. S. Bruning, "Improved Productivity and Job Satisfaction Through Employee Exercise Programs," *Hospital Material Management Quarterly* 9 (1988): 62–69; L. R. Gettman, "The Effect of Employee Physical Fitness on Job Performance," *Personnel Administration* (November 1980): 41–61.

4. For more discussion of the benefits of being fit, see K. H. Cooper, *It's Better to Believe* (Nashville, TN: Thomas Nelson, Inc., 1995). The paperback edition of this citation is K. H. Cooper, *Faith-Based Fitness* (Nashville, TN: Thomas Nelson, Inc., 1997).

5. For an in-depth discussion of research on physical activity and psychological outcomes, see "Physical Activity and Psychological Benefits: Internal Society of Sport Psychology Position Statement," *The Physician and Sports Medicine* 20, no. 10 (1992): 179–184; J. E. Brandon and J. M. Loftin, "Relationship of Fitness to Depression, State and Trait Anxiety, Internal Health Locus of Control, and Self-Control," *Perceptual and Motor Skills* 73, no. 2 (1991): 563–566.

6. These remarks appear in Rippe, op. cit.

7. See A. M. Paolone, et al., "Results of Two Years of Exercise Training in Middle-Aged Men," *The Physician and Sports Medicine* (December 1976): 77 D. Ornish, S. E. Brown, L. W. Scherwitz, et al., "Can Lifestyle Changes Reverse Coronary Heart Disease?," *Lancet* 336 (July, 1990), 21: 129–133; Smolin and Grossvenor, op. cit.

8. Healthy People 2000: National Health Promotion and Disease Prevention Objectives. Washington, DC: U.S. Department of Health and Human Services, 1990.

9. For a more precise discussion of these landmark studies, see E. E. Calle, E. Eugenia, M. J. Thun, J. M. Petrelli, et al., "Body-Mass Index and Mortality in a Prospective Cohort of U.S. Adults," *The New England Journal of Medicine* 341 (1999): 1097–1105; S. N. Blair, H. W. Kohl, R. S. Paffenbarger, Jr., D. G. Clark, K. H. Cooper, and L. W. Gibbons, "Physical Fitness and All-Cause Mortality: A Prospective Study of Healthy Men and Women," *Journal of the American Medical Association* 262, no. 17 (1989): 2395–2401; S. N. Blair, H. W. Kohl, C. E. Barlow, R. S. Paffenbarger, Jr., L. W. Gibbons, and C. A. Macera, "Changes in Physical Fitness and All-Cause Mortality. A Prospective Study of Healthy and Unhealthy Men," *Journal of the American Medical Association* 273, no. 14 (1995): 1093–1098.

10. C. Romano, "In Sickness and in Health," *Management Review* 83, no. 5 (1994): 40–46.

11. "Economic Cost of Cardiovascular Diseases," American Heart Association World Wide Web page, (americanheart.org/statistics/10econom.html), accessed February 2, 2003.

12. Health Education Branch, Office of Prevention, Education, and Control; National Heart, Lung, and Blood Institute, U.S. Department of Health and Human Services, Public Health Service, National Institutes of Health, *Cardiovascular Primer for the Workplace*, NIH Publication No. 81-2210, January, 1981.

13. This quotation is documented in C. Hymovitz, "Need to Boost Morale?", *Wall Street Journal*, 28 May 2002, sec. B1, p. 28.

14. More details related to this survey can be found in ibid.; J. Leinfelder, "Executive Training: How Five Managers Keep That Lean and Hungry Look," *Corporate Report-Minnesota* 22, no. 5 (1991): 86–93; Rippe, op. cit.

15. The fitness examples of executives have been documented in D. Jones, "Many Successful Women Also Athletic," *USA TODAY*, 26 March 2002, sec. 1B.; K. Hannon, "USA Today Profile: Charles Rossotti," *USA TODAY*, 17 February 1999, sec. 7B; A. J. Michels, "Doctor's Orders: CEOs of Pharmaceutical Companies Stay Fit Through Exercise and a Healthy Diet," *Fortune* 125, no. 12 (15 June 1992): 13–15; S. Kilman, "Sears Names as Chief Financial Officer Day, Who Helped Revive Safeway Inc." *Wall Street Journal*, 5 March 1999, sec. B-8.

16. This argument that "executives who are dedicated to fitness may be basing their exercise and diet routines on obsolete or incomplete data" was another finding from the survey of executives from the United States' top 3,000 companies (see endnote 15). Also see Rippe, op. cit., for more information on this survey and this particular finding from this survey.

The Journey Completed

*We must not cease from exploration and the end
of all our exploring will be to arrive where we began
and to know the place for the first time.*

—T. S. ELIOT

He set out on the journey with the best of intentions and with true determination. He would discover the place of peace, contentment, and fulfillment. This wonderful land was out there: He would find it and then return to his hopeful, hard-working people and bring them, too. Then all would at last be released from their toil-laden and imperfect existence.

He traveled long and hard; he crossed vast deserts and the highest of snowcapped mountains; he fought with wild beasts and defended himself against strange and hostile peoples. Still he could not find the wonderful land for which he searched.

At last, one day many years later, he wearily entered a land that seemed somehow peaceful. It was pleasant to look upon, and yes, the people were quite friendly. Somehow the land seemed new, yet comfortably familiar. He enjoyed himself for several days while he recovered from his long travels and regained his clarity of perspective.

Then one morning, having significantly recovered his faculties, the strangest of sensations went through him. This land had seemed familiar because it was the home that he had left behind so many years before. The people had not recognized him because of his greatly increased age and weather-worn features. Once realizing who he was, they were in a state of excitement and curiosity to know of the wonderful land of peace, contentment, and fulfillment that he must surely have discovered after so many years. They had waited so long for his return so that they too, might go there. Slowly the man responded to their questions. "Yes," he said, "there is a wonderful land and I have discovered it. It is not as I thought, though. You see, to go there is to be *here*—we were there all along but did not see."

"Well then, you have wasted many years and our hopes have been in vain," the people cried. "And look at you—you are but a shell of the fine physical specimen you were when you left."

"It is true," said the man. "I have traded many years of my life and a large portion of my physical strength for the realization that the wonderful land I sought in vain was mine all along. But I say to you, it is the best exchange I have ever made. You too can enjoy the contentment that I now know if you will but travel, not foolishly as I did, but with your mind into your heart so that you might know your soul."

We have now completed our journey together, and we hope you have found it worthwhile. Before you lay this book aside, though, we would like you to consider a few more ideas. The following discussion addresses personal effectiveness—what it is and where it comes from. Also, this closing chapter will consider briefly how to go about improving your world by contributing to the self-leadership of others, and it includes some thoughts concerning self-leadership possibilities for the future.

PERSONAL EFFECTIVENESS

"Tell me, oh great one, why are you so triumphant and able in your every endeavor?" asked the admirer.

"It is because I believe that I am so," he responded in a powerful and confident tone of voice.

"But then tell me, great one, why do you believe you are so triumphant and able?"

"Because I *am*," he responded confidently.

At this the admirer scratched his head and thought for awhile. Then he asked, "Are you triumphant and able because you *believe* you are so, or just because you *are*?"

At this question he turned to the admirer with a faint trace of a smile on his face and a gleam in his eye that said the admirer had asked well. Then he said, "Yes, I have already told you so."

Some key self-leadership ideas have been presented in this book. It should be clear that to be effective self-leaders, we need to recognize our interdependent relationships with the world in which we live, as well as the way we influence ourselves directly. Indeed, we largely create our own personal world through our actions, and our world acts on us in countless ways. We also need to recognize the importance of our mental as well as our physical behavior. The observable actions we take to deal with problems and challenges are important, but our thoughts about these challenges (mental behavior) are just as important.

A wide range of approaches is available to us to practice systematic self-leadership effectively. Several techniques can be used, such as self-observation, self-goal-setting, purpose examination, and self-reward, to help us accomplish what we need to accomplish but have a hard time getting ourselves to do. We also can tap into the natural enjoyment of our challenges by building into our efforts and otherwise seeking what we naturally enjoy about our activities. In particular, by facilitating a sense of competence, self-control, and purpose, the performance of naturally rewarding activities can truly serve as an effective self-leadership technique. In addition, an especially powerful approach involves essentially redesigning our psychological world by developing desirable patterns of thought through the development of constructive beliefs, self-talk, and imagery. Ultimately, all this should help us become effective self-leaders and achieve personal effectiveness.

What *is* personal effectiveness? It varies from person to person, but some basic aspects of personal effectiveness can be distinguished for most situations. We would describe persons as being personally effective, for example, if they are able to reasonably accomplish what they set out to do with their lives, if they develop a healthy belief in their capabilities and value as persons, and if they develop a fundamental and fairly stable satisfaction with life. To be personally effective is to believe we can deal with life's many challenges and enjoy the successful handling of them.

One insightful view of the ingredients to personal effectiveness is encompassed in a concept known as "self-efficacy."[1] Self-efficacy is, in essence, our level of effectiveness in dealing with our world. More specifically, our perceptions of our own ability to deal successfully with and overcome situations and challenges we face in life can have a major impact on our performance. Available evidence indicates that our self-efficacy judgments influence the activities we choose to undertake or avoid, how much effort we expend, and how long we will persist in the face of difficult situations. Low self-efficacy judgments (e.g., beliefs that we lack the ability to deal with a difficult challenge) can lead us to exaggerate mentally our own deficiencies and the potential hazards of difficult situations. This, in turn, can lead to anxiety and stress, and can detract from our performance. Our focus, for example, can too easily become that of obstacles and potential failure rather than opportunities and potentially successful alternative courses of action.

Perceptions of self-efficacy can indeed have an important influence on our personal effectiveness, but from where do our self-efficacy judgments come? Our self-efficacy judgments stem from several sources. One source is *observation* of the performance of others and their successes and failures. If we observe others with whom we can reasonably identify as they successfully overcome a particular challenge (earn a college degree, learn to skydive, etc.), our own self-efficacy judgments concerning the type of challenge involved should be enhanced. Another source is verbal *persuasion*. An inspiring speech by an athletic coach or a boss at work sometimes can convince the listeners that they can succeed and move them to execute the action necessary to do so. A third source stems from our perceptions of our *physical reactions* to a situation. If we feel calm and relaxed in the face of a challenge, for example, we are more likely to judge ourselves capable of overcoming the challenge than if we feel anxious and stressful.

Each of these sources of our self-efficacy perceptions is important and provides us with useful insight for enhancing our personal effectiveness. If we seek out people with whom we can identify (people we believe are reasonably equal in ability to us), who use their talents well and overcome challenges they face, we provide ourselves with a good source for developing positive judgments of our own self-efficacy. Similarly, purposefully exposing ourselves to constructive verbal persuasion and gaining control over our physical reactions to difficulties can help us improve our self-perceptions, which should facilitate our performance. The most important source of perceptions of self-efficacy, however, is even more basic. It is simply our own *performance history*. If we experience successes in difficult situations, our perceptions of our self-efficacy will be improved. If we experience failure, they will be undermined.

This bit of information provides us with the basis for a valuable insight—that personal effectiveness leads to personal effectiveness. If we can master self-leadership skills such as those suggested in this book and consequently successfully take control of our

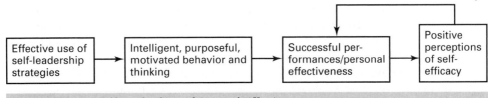

FIGURE 11-1   Self-Leadership and Personal Effectiveness

lives and our situations, we can enhance our current and future performance—our current performance through more intelligent, purposeful, and motivated immediate thought and behavior, and our future performance through enhanced self-perceptions of our personal efficacy or, in essence, of our own effectiveness. Thus, if we believe we are personally effective, we are likely to become even more so. The best way to develop a positive belief in our own effectiveness is by handling the challenges we face in life successfully. Mastery of systematic self-leadership skills can help us achieve personal excellence in our own lives.

These ideas are illustrated in Figure 11-1. Self-leadership skills are an instrumental part of our level of personal effectiveness. They impact on our performance capability directly by helping motivate and guide us in our immediate performances, and in future performances through the effect on our self-efficacy perceptions.

SOME ADDITIONAL THOUGHTS

Before closing this book, two additional issues will be considered: first, some tips on developing the self-leadership skills of others, and second, thoughts on self-leadership issues of the future.

SUPERLEADERSHIP: LEADING OTHERS TO LEAD THEMSELVES[2]

"All right, Private Barnes. What's on your mind?"

"With all due respect, Sergeant Rogers, sir, I don't understand your leadership methods."

"O.K., Barnes—get it off your chest. What is it that's bothering you? You can speak frankly with me—you know that."

"Well, sir, it's just that we have one of the best outfits around. We always get a top rating and get the job done. But it seems we men do it all ourselves. Sure, you give guidelines, but you always want *us* to make the decisions. We are even supposed to reward and discipline ourselves! Don't get me wrong—I don't like being kicked around like most of the other sergeants do to get their men going; it just seems that you place too much responsibility on us enlisted men. After all, you're the officer and this 'you're your own sergeant in my outfit and I expect you to do a good job of making yourself the best soldier you can be' stuff you always give us seems funny, somehow. I mean, *you're* the leader, aren't you? Why do you want *us* to take all the responsibility for ourselves? It's like we're all supposed to be leaders around here. It's like we've *got* to be because you won't be one." Barnes paused nervously, his heart pounding, afraid he had said too much.

But Sergeant Rogers seemed unshaken. "Tell me, private. How do you and the men feel about yourselves?"

"Well, damn good, sir," he started cautiously. "We *ought* to—we're the best," he continued, now more confidently. "We pull together, supporting one another all the time. Yet each of us has a sort of individual dignity. We believe in ourselves and we do a hell of a job in our work."

"You were in the service a while before you got in my outfit, Barnes—how did you feel then?"

"Well, not too good, I guess. Being a soldier can kind of get you down. All I ever heard about is what I was doing wrong. I felt kind of like a rat in a maze with a hot electric wire chasing me." Then Barnes caught himself, "But at least the other sergeants would tell me what to do—they'd make the decisions and I would just do the work," he said quickly.

"Well, that's not the way I operate, private. I used to, but I don't anymore. Somewhere in my past I discovered the tremendous potential of every man, and I don't want to waste it anymore."

Now Barnes was in deep reflection. After a while a faint smile came to his face as though he had just discovered something new and wonderful. "I guess you lead us to lead ourselves, sir," he said (as much to himself as he did to Sergeant Rogers). "It's funny—you even got me to answer my own question," he said almost under his breath while turning to leave.

"Barnes," the sergeant called, stopping him in mid-stride, "you know I'm proud of you men."

"We know, sir," Barnes responded, "we are too, and I thank you for that."

The important interrelationship between ourselves and our world has been discussed consistently throughout this book. In addition, Chapters 3 and 4 suggested that for us to enjoy an activity naturally, one important aspect of the activity is that it provide us with a sense of purpose, which in many cases is encompassed in the notion of altruism. Here we would like to suggest a powerful method for improving our personal world and achieving a sense of altruistic purpose at the same time: the practice of SuperLeadership. SuperLeadership can be described as the process of helping others develop and practice systematic effective self-leadership. It involves bringing out and stimulating the development of personal effectiveness of people with whom we associate. Although Henry Sims and Charles Manz wrote an entire book on this topic entitled *SuperLeadership* (see Note 2), the idea of leading others to lead themselves is a unique and compelling perspective on the broader topic of leadership itself. Here are a few simple ideas and a procedure, which will be suggested as a starting point.

Henry Sims and Charles Manz suggested a procedure for managers to help their employees manage themselves better.[3] It consisted of three primary components: setting a good example, guidance, and reinforcement of self-management. The first step is displaying self-leadership skills in your own behavior. It has been said that "actions speak louder than words," and in this case that old adage is especially true. By displaying systematic self-leadership practice in your behavior (setting goals for yourself, purposefully making your work naturally enjoyable, seeking out opportunities rather than shrinking in the face of obstacles, etc.), you are serving as an effective, concrete model and stimulus for others to do the same.

Providing an example for others, however, is not enough. They also will likely need a considerable amount of specific guidance. Here encouragement and instruction in self-leadership skills are important. The goal is to get the target of your efforts thinking and behaving in a self-leading manner appropriate to that person. One useful approach to accomplishing this end is to ask appropriate questions: Do you have any goals for your efforts? How well do you think you did, and how do you feel about that? What aspects of your work do you enjoy? How could you make it more enjoyable? What kinds of opportunities are you pursuing right now? Are you looking for new ones?

When they *do* start putting self-leadership techniques into practice, suggestions and feedback are important. In particular, positive reinforcement of self-leadership effort is crucial (e.g., "I'm glad to see you setting goals for yourself. This should help you better accomplish what you set out to do." "Your outlook has really improved. I can tell that opportunities, rather than obstacles, are your primary motivators now"). It's important to remember, though, that the aim is to shift the leadership function to the other person(s). SuperLeadership ultimately means assisting others to become their own primary source of goals, rewards, work enjoyment, opportunities, and so forth in a way that is best suited to them. In their book *The New SuperLeadership*, Manz and Sims provide specific strategies for developing self-leadership in individuals, as well as in teams and in broader organizational cultures (see Note 2). Whether the others are work subordinates, a spouse, a child, or a friend, ideally the aim should be to help them become all they are capable of becoming in a way that will give them the most personal satisfaction and growth.

The Ultimate SuperLeader:
A Short Personal Essay About the Parent as Leader

—Henry P. Sims. Jr

I thought I would share with you a few ideas that have emerged as a part of my thinking over the past few years: the notion that the ultimate SuperLeader opportunity is that of parent. More specifically, in a few paragraphs, I'll attempt to articulate a few thoughts about the parent as "leader" and the child as "follower."

First, let's cover some basic definitions. **Leadership** is a process of influencing others—often, but not necessarily, in a hierarchical relationship. Leadership is often expressed through coordinated patterns of behaviors, which we sometimes call leadership types or styles. The four types that I typically discuss most are: (1) **Directive** (or, **Strong Man**), (2) **Transactor**, (3) **Transformational** (or, **Visionary Hero**), and **Empowering** (or, **SuperLeader**). Most readers will recognize this typology as an extension of the popular transactor/transformation theoretical perspective.

(continued)

Since this essay is mainly about SuperLeadership, let me define this type of leadership. **SuperLeadership is leading others to lead themselves.** SuperLeaders aim to create followers who are adept at self-leadership, so it is mainly a type intended to develop others. It is not laissez-faire leadership, but an active form of leadership that uses modeling, guided participation, and delegation to provide opportunities for enhancing self-leadership. A SuperLeader often arranges for a follower to have a mastery experience, where one successfully performs a set of behaviors for the first time. SuperLeadership is not mutually exclusive with transactor or transformational leadership.

Certainly, a parent has a role of responsibility and authority over a child as the child ages and matures. The responsibility is complete and total at the infant stage, and gradually diminishes (though not in a linear function) as the child grows and becomes an adult. At about age 18 or so, our society and culture generally recognize that the parent's responsibility has declined to a low point . . . perhaps even zero. At this final stage, the child has relatively little legal, formal, or necessarily cultural role as a "follower" of the parent.

As the child grows and matures, a parent fulfills their leadership role toward the child through the parent's behavior—behavior that is intended to influence the thoughts, values, beliefs, and behavior of the child. Most of all, any parent has a **choice** of **how** they wish to "lead" the child. One way to think about this choice is to consider that the parent can express leadership through various patterns of behavior that we typically think of as leadership types, or styles. Following are some brief thoughts about how various leadership types might be expressed.

For example, the parent might act as a "strong man," or directive/authoritarian toward the child. Parenting through this type would entail influence through instruction, command, directive, assigned goals, and perhaps punishment. Requiring a child to have a "time out" in response to unruly or bad behavior is an example of the use of strong man leadership.

A parent might act as a "transactor" in an attempt to control adolescent behavior. That is, the parent would use rewards to influence behavior. The implicit message is: "Do it the way I want you to, and I'll give you privileges and rewards that you desire."

Certainly many parents want to act as a "visionary hero" toward their offspring. We hope to inspire them toward a life or career vision that, as experienced adults, we see as productive, useful, contributory, and happy.

Finally, the last leadership option is the idea of behaving as a "SuperLeader." With this type of leadership, we attempt to provide the child with a series of "mastery experiences" that will enable them to be an effective self-leader—one who has the capacity to successfully make their own decisions about such life issues as smoking, alcohol and drugs, sexual behavior, emotional relationships, personal work ethic, and so on.

I must confess that in my own experience with three children, I have at one time or another used all of these forms of leadership, with varying degrees of success. (I'm tempted to say various degrees of failure!) I have used "time out" to control unacceptable toddler behavior. My strong man leadership typically had a useful short-term effect, but wasn't very good in really changing behavior.

I admit to using bribery on occasion—a form of transactor leadership. Again, this approach usually produces a short-term result, but then creates a demand effect of constant use of the reward in order to lead. If the reward is not forthcoming, then the behavior does not persist.

I have always tried to be a "visionary hero"—to inspire and articulate noble life goals and aspirations. In the short term, this often seemed fruitless. Interestingly, however, I believe this leadership approach does have longer-term effects, and sometimes can influence child behavior much, much later in subtle ways. Most of all, visionary hero leadership is very important for conveying fundamental beliefs and values. The danger is that too vigorous or persistent use of visionary hero leadership can be overcontrolling and can create a backlash.

Finally, it seems reasonable to me that in the end, SuperLeadership, or empowering leadership, is absolutely necessary. As a parent, I believe the most effective influence approach is to model one's own self-leadership to the child, and, moreover, to arrange opportunities for a child to experience those hundreds of mastery experiences along the journey of growth. After all, don't we really want children who can grow to adults fully capable of making their own decision about the important values of life?

Most of all, I believe this leadership role of parent is difficult and challenging. First, we have the problem of controlling our own behavior. How many times have I "intellectually" wanted to behave as a visionary or SuperLeader, and yet, I actually behave as a strong man? (More often than I would like to admit!) How many times have I failed to model behavior in myself that I desire for the child? Further, I believe the "variance" of a child's ultimate adult behavior that can be explained by a parent's leadership is limited. A child is subject to genetic disposition, and influence from many, many sources that are outside the parent's control. Even the best-intended and implemented parental leadership is sometimes not effective.

But I do believe that the potential of parental leadership is significant, and that if we accept the parental role, indeed we should attempt to lead our children. And, we must make choices about how we will lead. Most of the time, our leadership can produce a response, and occasionally we will experience great self-fulfillment when we observe our child's behavior. For me, the parenting is the ultimate SuperLeadership opportunity. For those of you who are just beginning this journey, it will indeed be a challenge and an adventure. I wish you success.

SOURCE: Copyright by Henry P. Sims, Jr., April 3, 2002, www.hanksims.com, accessed February 6, 2003.

It should be apparent from "A Tale of Self-Leadership" in Chapter 9 that a lot of Jen's self-leadership effectiveness (and Tom's ineffectiveness) stems from the way she leads her subordinates. Jen is an effective self-leadership model and allows her employees the freedom to exercise initiative. To emphasize further Jen's SuperLeadership style, let's return to her case as the tale continues.

The Tale Continued

In the months that passed under Jennifer Wilks's leadership, the department underwent many significant changes. Jen's innovative ideas often led to refinements in work processes, and efficiency continued to rise. These were the obvious changes, but the most important ones were less obvious and invariably involved the growth of her people. In fact, many of Jen's subordinates who never had been viewed previously as particularly innovative or self-directing had gradually evolved into creative, independent workers. Many of Jen's better ideas began with suggestions from her employees, or in some cases the whole idea would be designed and implemented by one or more of her employees with little or no involvement from Jen. Jen was quick to give them credit in front of their peers, as well as their superiors.

"Good morning on this beautiful, sunny day," Jen said to her staff at the beginning of one of their weekly department meetings. "I'd like to officially introduce Dave Henry to you, although I believe most of you have already met him. He joined us at the end of last week just having received his degree from City U. I, for one, am extremely pleased that Dave has decided to work with us, and I hope that each of you will help Dave during his transition.

"And, now, I believe it's Nancy's turn to conduct the meeting. So I'll stop rambling and turn the floor over to her," Jen finished.

The meeting was fairly typical, led by one of Jen's subordinates who rotated this responsibility. It began with a few minutes of brainstorming of department work improvements, followed by a practical discussion of department challenges that needed to be addressed. They were referred to as challenges or opportunities because Jen, early on after she had taken the department head position, had convinced her staff that problems were opportu-

nities that had not yet been adequately explored. Jen had in fact changed a lot of the old language in the department so that it projected more positive imagery. The transition occurred largely as a result of the example Jen had set in the early meetings of her tenure in the department. As a consequence, over time, the meetings themselves had become more pleasant and productive, and on this particular day, the tone of the meeting was the same with one exception.

"I know I'm pretty new around here, Bob," Dave, the new employee, was saying to one of the department staff, "but I think some real problems might occur in the implementation phase of your plan."

"I appreciate your interest, Dave, and I invite your input to help me work out some of the details. Also, Dave, you may find this a little strange, but we don't use the word *problem* much in meetings around here anymore. We've decided it has a negative effect on our thinking, so we try to talk in terms of *challenges* or *opportunities*."

"Oh," Dave responded in a slightly surprised tone. "Sorry about that," he said as he turned toward Jen with a mildly confused look on his face.

"Don't worry about it," Jen answered for Bob. "We know it takes some getting used to, but we think you'll like the positive atmosphere that's created by managing the language we use so that we create constructive imagery for problem solving or what we refer to as *opportunity generation*."

In fact, the whole meeting seemed a little strange to Dave, who couldn't understand what was so bad about identifying problems with ideas that were being considered in the department. After all, the first step in effective decision making he had been taught at City U is to identify the major problems that exist. Over time, though, he became a real supporter of the unique subculture in the department that reinforced employee initiative and being your own leader much more than avoiding mistakes. Dave found this took a lot of the negative stress out of the work and made it a fun environment in which to spend his time. In fact, a kind of informal slogan in the department said, "If you're not making any mistakes, you're probably not trying hard enough." It's not that making mistakes was encouraged, but exercising initiative and taking reasonable chances were expected in the department as a natural part of each person's contribution of their full enthusiastic (not just compliant) potential.

Dave especially learned this lesson the day he lost a major order from a potential client because he was late in delivering a price bid. His bid was late because he had taken a lot of time to develop a unique service arrangement tailored to the client's needs—the key to his proposal. After explaining the situation to Jen, he braced himself for the logical chewing out he would receive after such a screwup.

"How do you like your work here so far?" Jen began.

"Uh, fine," Dave responded, sounding a little confused about the question.

"Have you been redesigning your job to fit your interests and strengths?"

"I'm not sure. I haven't really thought about it," Dave said, sounding even more confused and unsure how to answer.

"Well, I hope you have been," Jen said. "I want you to get a real kick out of your work and to be able to put your best foot forward.

"Now, as for your proposal, why did you develop this new service plan?" Jen continued.

"To provide the best package for the client," Dave responded, "and the most attractive overall product for getting the contract."

"Why do you want the contract? What are you working toward?" Jen asked next.

"Well, I'm hoping to increase our contract volume for this product line," Dave answered.

"Good, I like people to be goal oriented. Have you thought about how much of an increase you're working toward?"

And so the conversation continued. "How well do you think you're doing?" "Do you celebrate your successes, reward yourself when you do well?" And as they talked, Dave was getting a sense of Jen's leadership style. Jen wanted her people to think, not only about how they did their work, but why. Most of all though, she just wanted her people to think about the choices they constantly faced and made. She wanted them to think about their personal effectiveness and skill in leading themselves, not just their technical proficiency.

"But, still, surely the lost contract was a significant failure and sooner or later the conversation will have to get around to my botched performance and a justifiable reproach from Jen," Dave thought to himself.

Jen continued to examine the report that Dave had prepared for the client for what seemed an awfully long time. Dave was sure Jen must be gathering her feelings of dissatisfaction for a pointed reprimand. "Congratulations," Jen said finally. "This is the most innovative service plan I've seen in this department thus far, and it capitalizes on our resource strengths very well. This is going to generate a lot of business for us with our clients in the future."

Now Dave looked confused. "You mean I've lost a large order with an important potential new client, and you're not mad?"

"Gee, Dave, you sound almost disappointed. You see, I don't believe in chewing someone out for initiative and hard work. Besides, I think what you see as a short-term failure is going to generate tremendous opportunities for us in the long run."

"Well, the client was pleased with the plan and told me that although it wasn't in on time to be considered for this order, he felt confident that we would be getting orders from them in the future."

"You see, I told you," Jen responded with a businesslike smile that indicated she already was anticipating the future benefits for the department.

"I guess you're right," Dave said with a slight smile now himself, although he still looked bewildered as he turned to leave Jen's office.

"By the way, Dave," Jen stopped him in midstride. "Don't expect me to chew you out every time you make a mistake. I suspect you'll know when you've screwed up, and I figure it's your job to keep yourself on track as well as your peers. Give your work your best shot making full use of your talents and I'm confident that you'll win a lot more than you lose. The longer you're around here, I think you'll find we all operate that way and it works."

And in the days ahead, Dave found Jen's observation to be true indeed. Dave, in fact, became one of the best self-leaders in the department, following Jen's example but also developing his own system of self-direction.

Once, several weeks later, when asked by a top corporate executive what made Jen such an effective department manager, Dave's response was quick and enthusiastic. "She lets us lead ourselves," Dave said simply. "And it's not hard to do around here with the example she sets and the encouragement she gives us," he continued. "I am still getting used to her style. I mean she still surprises me. Sometimes I think I've really blown it on a project and she praises me for my initiative, hard work, and creativity, even though things did not work out the way we hoped. Other times I think I've done something just the way she would have, the way I think she would want me to, and she sounds kind of disappointed that I didn't come up with a new, better way that is all my own. Jen likes us to get the credit and to have the satisfaction of succeeding—that's what pleases her."

Dave continued: "I guess you could say Jen has helped shape a uniquely effective little world here where yes men and women are not allowed, a place where people grow and develop and have a lot of fun because they have the satisfaction of testing the limits of their creativity and ability. It's funny, we are all leaders in this department. I'm still not sure how Jen has done it, but in my book she's the best. She's the best leader I've ever seen, and it seems like she is the best because she doesn't need to be. Jen wants us to fully share her leadership role and her glory by being our own ultimate leaders—each one of us. And she wants each of us to be the best self-leaders we can be."

The Tale in Perspective Continued

SuperLeadership is a real leadership alternative. Modeling, encouraging, guiding, and reinforcing self-leadership are the key ingredients. Jen does this; her employees benefit and so does her organization.

Jen clearly models effective self-leadership in her own behavior and serves as a credible example of personal effectiveness. She encourages her people to make choices that contribute to their personal growth, effectiveness, and satisfaction. She guides them in their development with strategic use of questions that stimulate self-leadership thinking. She also reinforces constructive self-leadership practice, sometimes even when immediate performance does not measure up. Jen does this because she realizes that in the long run, fully developed, enthusiastic, self-led workers will win a lot more than they lose and a lot more than if they are just compliant followers of her commands.

Finally, Jen has developed a subculture in which self-leadership can feed on itself—one in which people are challenged to be all they can be and know that what is expected is nothing less. Jen has, in essence, facilitated the emergence of an almost idyllic world for fully utilizing human resources. Yet it's a world that is achievable for those leaders who are willing to let their people share in the process and learn the exhilaration of mastering the leadership of themselves. ■

Future Directions in Self-Leadership

He looked carefully into the eyes of the very intelligent being from another world. Then he asked, "Do you think we on earth are primitive?"

"No," the being answered, "at least not in all ways."

"Then you do think we are primitive in *some* ways," he continued, intending the statement as a question. But the being did not respond. "I mean," he continued, "we have explored the universe, and we have harnessed the power of the atom. We have made great advances in the control of disease, and we have even mastered the art of manipulating genes for improving our race in future generations. Given all this, how can you think we are primitive in some way? In what way?" he asked now in an irritated voice.

"Yes, you have explored much," the being responded. "In some ways you have even surpassed the beings of my planet in your mastery of the physical world, though not many."

The man shook his head in acknowledgment. "But also you have neglected much."

"What do you mean? What have we neglected?" the human asked.

"Your focus has been outward. You have neglected what is within. It's as though you have tried to master living but have forgotten to explore life."

"What do you mean? We have made great advances in biology and medicine. We are closer to controlling life itself than we have ever been!" he responded a bit too emphatically.

"I'm not talking about your physical bodies," continued the being. "I'm talking about the core of life, the mind and the spirit."

"But we've made great advances in psychology and psychiatry, and tremendous discoveries regarding the functioning of the brain," exclaimed the human.

"The brain is but a part of the physical body—a sort of computer to be used in dealing with the world. Life is more. You have spent so much time trying to control the world that you have forgotten the mastery of yourselves."

"But science indicates that we are ultimately what the world makes us through evolution, socialization, and so forth. It is the world that makes us what we are, isn't it?" the man asked, now thoughtfully—unsure, as though he was beginning to understand. "Isn't that the true order of things and why we must focus our major efforts on the world?"

"Only if you choose it to be," the being answered simply. "We of my planet have chosen to focus our primary efforts inward instead of outward. We have discovered that the world is largely what we make it. But we must first make something of ourselves before we can make the world. Yes, you have surpassed us in some things: weaponry to destroy and instruments to squeeze from the physical world the wants of the body. In this way you are advanced. But you have neglected the most powerful resource you have—the power of the mind, the core of yourselves."

As a final consideration, it is useful to look for a moment into an imaginary crystal ball of self-leadership possibilities for the future. Our belief is that the major break-throughs in the next few decades will be in an arena that we generally have thought of as a bit strange and almost mystic. We are referring to the capabilities and powers we hold deep within ourselves but that are largely unexplored and uncharted as of yet: the powers of the mind.[4]

An interesting and insightful book on the subject is Barbara Brown's *Supermind*.[5] She argues that the brain and the mind are two distinct realities. Considerable effort has been spent exploring the physical functioning of the brain: electrochemical impulses, left and right hemisphere functioning, and so forth. Our understanding of the almost-mysti-cal powers of the mind, however, seems to have been reserved for usually questionable and unscientific witnessing from persons encountering strange experiences that defy sci-entific explanation: people lifting cars off endangered loved ones, miraculous physical healings through effort of mind, premonitions, and extra sensory perception (ESP).

Yet the evidence is vast enough and often credible enough to warrant a belief that mind power is a strong, perhaps the most powerful, untapped resource. Take, for ex-ample, the mounting evidence regarding biofeedback—a process by which persons are connected to sophisticated monitors of the human bodily functions that provide feed-back regarding physical processes that, in the past, were considered beyond the arena of intentional control. Experience with biofeedback has shown that not only can we control bodily functions such as heartbeat, blood pressure, and skin surface tempera-ture, but also brain wave activity. The point is that through a learning process, humans can control processes of the body (even brain activity) that for years were believed to be beyond control.

In this book, we have attempted to balance the emphasis placed on physical behavior with thought. Both play an important role in the total self-leadership picture. In the future, however, self-leadership advances will need to travel beyond the level of our current conscious awareness capability into the largely unconscious processes and powers of the mind. The purpose is not so much to use the mind as a window to our "true personalities," as Freud and other psychologists have done in the past, but instead as a resource for gaining advanced self-leadership capability and personal effectiveness. Preliminary journeys have begun into this exciting new frontier. The ulti-mate in personal effectiveness of the future will likely be an advanced state of integra-tion and harmony of our world, our behavior, our conscious thought processes, and the deeper recesses of the mind.

Before we end this chapter, we'd like you to consider the story of the koi, an inter-esting fish, also referred to as the Japanese carp. The amazing thing about the koi is that if you keep it in a small container, the fish will only attain 2 to 3 inches in length. If you put it in a larger bowl or a small pond, it will grow 6 to 10 inches long. However, when placed in a huge body of water where it can expand without confinement, it has the potential to reach sizes of 36 to 48 inches in length.

The story of the koi clearly illustrates that the growth of this fish is strongly related to the size of its world. In a similar light, we feel that the size of a person's "pond"—the mental world in which she or he lives—can truly impact whether one fully develops in all aspects of life. We hope the ideas that encompass self-leadership help you expand your world, remove the limits that you may have placed on what you believe you can accomplish, and grow to realize the enormous potential that exists inside of you.

Notes

1. See Albert Bandura, *Self-Efficacy: The Exercise of Control* (New York: W. H. Freeman & Co., 1997).

2. This is the title of the book by Charles C. Manz and Henry P. Sims, Jr. (San Francisco: Berrett-Koehler, 2001) on the subject of leadership of others to become self-leaders.

3. See Manz and Sims, *The New SuperLeadership;* C. Manz and H. Sims, Jr., *Company of Heroes* (New York: Wiley, 1996); and Charles Manz and Henry P. Sims, Jr., "Self-Management as a Substitute for Leadership: A Social Learning Theory Perspective," *Academy of Management Review* 5 (1980): 361–367. See also Donald Meichenbaum and Roy Cameron, "The Clinical Potential of Modifying What Clients Say to Themselves" in M. J. Mahoney and C. E. Thoresen, *Self-Control: Power to the Person* (Monterey, CA: Brooks/Cole, 1974), which provided us with the basis for the procedure.

4. An interesting book on using the power of the mind is authored by Paule R. Scheele, *Natural Brilliance: Moving from Feeling Stuck to Achieving Success* (Wayzata, MN: Learning Strategies Corporation, 1997).

5. Barbara B. Brown, *Supermind: The Ultimate Energy* (New York: Harper & Row, 1980).

Epilogue

It is only with the heart that one can see rightly;
what is essential is invisible to the eye.

—Antoine De Saint-Ex

Having completed our writing, we have found it interesting to read back through what we have written. It has been a useful time of reflection regarding our own self-leadership. We have not yet mastered all the self-leadership strategies suggested in this book, but we have used many of them successfully, and we are continually working on others. We have come to realize that we wrote this book as much for ourselves as we did for others. The significant time and energy we have spent over the past decade studying, thinking, and reading about self-leadership necessitated that we attempt to organize a coherent, workable framework for application. In a way, the framework we have presented represents a personal goal for our own style of living.

Through our reflection, we also have come to another perhaps even more important realization: Although we already knew we have much to learn from others, we now see that we also have a great deal to learn from ourselves. The rather philosophical thought has occurred to us that possibly there is a basic truth regarding our own lives deep within us, and this truth specifies our most suitable style for living. Maybe that's a large part of what self-leadership is all about: seeking that part of ourselves that best defines a satisfactory fabric with which to weave our life experiences into a personally effective life. The ideas we have presented in this book (most of which have been applied successfully in multiple settings) represent our best attempt at providing a vehicle to help you (and ourselves) embark on such a journey. In closing, we truly hope our words have benefited you in some manner. We hope the self-leadership principles discussed throughout this book will help you achieve your grandest goals and your most delightful dreams. We leave you with the following poem to ponder. It is hoped that self-leadership will be the catalyst toward helping you "start your somedays, today"!

Start Your Somedays . . . Today!
Have you ever put something off
Because the timing wasn't just exact?
Maybe you refused to take that first step
As fear stopped you in your tracks.

How about refusing to begin your dreams,
Putting things off for a while.
Have you ever said, "Maybe tomorrow?"
Have you ever said, "Someday I'll?"

Consider the intelligent lady
With the ability to make good grades.
She said she'd further her education
Once the bills were paid.

Or how about the older gentleman
Who wanted to travel the world around.
He said he'd begin his journey
Once his schedule began to slow down.

What about the aspiring young lad
Who had that novel written—in his mind.
He said he'd put it on paper
Whenever he could possibly find the time.

And finally, that love-struck person
With secret admiration for that guy.
She would let him know her true feelings
When she wasn't feeling all that shy.

The message of these examples,
I hope, is crystal clear.
The time to start your aspirations
Is now—not next year.

Because the bills might never get paid,
Your schedule won't slow down,
Extra time won't somehow appear,
Complete confidence won't be found.

So if you wait to take all those risks
Until all the signals say, "Go,"
Your "someday I'lls" will never come;
Your dreams, you'll never know.

So begin that job or go back to school.
Start to smile and remove that frown.
"Because sometimes you have to jump off that cliff;
And build your wings—on the way down."

SOURCE: Christopher Neck, *Medicine for the Mind: Healing Words to Help You Soar* (New York: McGraw-Hill, 1996).

Index